New Flavours

LIGHTER AND HEALTHIER FINE DINING AT HOME

ELAINE ELLIOT AND VIRGINIA LEE

Photography by Julian Beveridge

FORMAC PUBLISHING COMPANY LIMITED
HALIFAX 1997

We wish to acknowledge the contributions from the following Inns and Restaurants of the Atlantic region.

Acton's Grill & Café, Wolfville, NS
Amherst Shore Country Inn, Lorneville, NS
The Algonquin Hotel, Saint Andrews, NB
Auberge Le Vieux Presbytere De Bouctouche 1880
 Ltée, Bouctouche, NB
Bellhill Tea House & Gift Shop, Canning, NS
Blomidon Inn, Wolfville, NS
Bluenose Lodge, Lunenburg, NS
Braeside Inn, Pictou, NS
Charlotte Lane Café & Crafts, Shelburne, NS
Chez Françoise, Shediac, NB
Chez la Vigne Restaurant, Wolfville, NS
Compass Rose Inn, Lunenburg, NS
Cooper's Inn & Restaurant, Shelburne, NS
The Doctor's Inn, Thyne Valley, PEI
Duncreigan Country Inn, Mabou, NS
The Dunes Café, Brackley Beach, PEI
The Galley, Marriots Cove, NS
Haddon Hall, Chester, NS
Halliburton House Inn, Halifax, NS
Inn at Bay Fortune, Bay Fortune, PEI
Inn on the Cove, Saint John, NB
Inn on the Lake, Waverley, NS
Keltic Lodge, Ingonish, NS

The Lion Inn, Lunenburg, NS
Little Shemogue Country Inn, Little Shemogue, NB
The Marshlands Inn, Sackville, NB
Off Broadway Café, Charlottetown, PEI
The Palliser, Truro, NS
The Pansy Patch, St. Andrews, NB
The Pines Resort Hotel, Digby, NS
Planters' (Barracks) Country Inn, Starrs Point, NS
Quaco Inn, St. Martins, NB
Quarterdeck Beachside Villas & Grill, Summerville
 Beach, NS
The Salmon River House Country Inn, Salmon River,
 NS
Seasons in Thyme, Thyne Valley, PEI
The Shadow Lawn Country Inn, Rothesay, NB
Steamers Stop Inn, Gagetown, NB
Sunshine Café, Antigonish, NS
Sweet Basil Bistro, Halifax, NS
Tattingstone Inn, Wolfville, NS
Unni's, Halifax, NS
The Walker Inn, Pictou, NS
West Point Lighthouse, West Point, PEI
White Point Beach Lodge & Resort, Hunts Point, NS
The Whitman Inn, Caledonia, NS

Dedication:

This book is dedicated to our husbands, Robert and Mel, and to our families, with love.

Canadian Cataloguing in Publication Data
Elliot, Elaine, 1939-
        New flavours: lighter and healthier dining at home.
        (Maritime flavours)
        ISBN 0-88780-408-X
1. Low-fat diet — Recipes. 2. Cookery, Canadian — Maritime Provinces. I.
Lee, Virginia, 1947- II. Beveridge, Julian. III. Title. IV. Title: New flavours:
lighter and healthier dining at home. V. Series.
RM219.E44 1997   641.5'638   C97-950007-9

Formac Publishing Company Limited
5502 Atlantic Street
Halifax, N.S.
B3H 1G4

CONTENTS

From: PEI
My trip to Prince
Edward Island for
the 25th yr. of the
Terry Fox Run on
the Confederation
Bridge.

INTRODUCTION

Following the success of our Maritime Flavours series of cookbooks, we were invited by our publisher to explore the trend towards lighter, healthier and more innovative dining in the Maritimes. With this quest in mind, we travelled to the finest inns and restaurants in the region. Again and again, we found that while today's diners are more cosmopolitan in their tastes, they are ever mindful of maintaining a healthy diet. And, as we had suspected, we discovered that the chefs of the Maritimes reflect this trend in their delicious and innovative cuisine.

Today, chefs across the Maritimes are influenced by a shrinking globe that provides easy access to many exotic products. As a result, our "traditional" cuisine is undergoing radical change. Chefs are not afraid to take the best products from other areas of the world and marry them to our local specialties.

Where else but in the Maritimes could you find Bay of Fundy mussels served in a spicy Thai sauce or grilled Atlantic salmon infused with green peppercorns? Without compromising flavour, our chefs are preparing lighter and healthier menus, and they were pleased to share their recipes with us. Be warned, however: this focus on lighter, healthier and more innovative dishes does not preclude a few decadent variations. We can't help but be naughty once in a while!

After much selection, consultation, home-testing and satisfying discovery, we are certain that we have pulled together a collection of truly innovative and mouthwatering recipes. The book features dishes for every occasion and course, from from appetizers to entrees to desserts. We are particularly excited about including a section on condiments, many of which complement a variety of dishes and add colour, texture and pizazz to the simplest of meals. In addition, in our luncheon section, you will find delicious choices for a vegetarian diet.

The recipes in this collection all come from the kitchens of the region's top chefs; at the same time, they have been carefully tested and adjusted for the ease of the home cook. They generally serve four to six people, and most ingredients are readily available in supermarkets. A few ingredients are more exotic, but can be easily found in specialty stores.

This book would not be complete without thank-yous to all those who have helped us put it together. In particular, we would like to thank our photographer, Julian Beveridge, for expertly capturing the creativity of our chefs; and, of course, we once again extend our gratitude to all our contributors from within the hospitality industry. Thank you for your expertise, creativity and generosity.

Finally, to all our readers in the Maritimes and elsewhere, we offer this book. Enjoy!

Elaine Elliot & Virginia Lee

APPETIZERS

Appetizers are often the easiest dishes with which to experiment because they are small and do not constitute the main body of the meal. The entrance of the appetizer whets the appetite with a small sampling of what to expect from the courses to follow. Our chefs of the Maritimes have offered us a variety of recipes that we are sure you will want to try.

The chef from The Whitman Inn suggests you step out into your garden and snip off a few squash or zucchini blossoms, not for a floral arrangement but to serve to your unsuspecting guests! Mark Gabrieau from the Sunshine Café shares his recipe for a robust Italian Bruschetta, while Ross Mavis of the Inn on the Cove offers a healthy mid-Eastern Hummus Dip.

◀ *Tattingstone Smoked Mackerel*

TATTINGSTONE-STYLE SMOKED MACKEREL

TATTINGSTONE INN

Chef Gustavo Bautista developed this innovative appetizer using distinctively Maritime smoked mackerel. At Tattingstone Inn, he also serves it as an hors d'oeuvre canape for larger crowds.

1/2 pound smoked mackerel
1/4 medium green pepper, finely chopped
1/4 medium red pepper, finely chopped
1/2 medium red onion, finely chopped
2-3 tablespoons mayonnaise
1/2 teaspoon horseradish
1/2 tablespoon capers, chopped
1/2 teaspoon Worcestershire sauce
1 teaspoon lemon juice

Shred mackerel with fingers, removing bones and skin. Combine mackerel with peppers, onion, horseradish, capers, Worcestershire and lemon juice. Gently toss with mayonnaise, adding only enough mayonnaise to bind mixture together. Cover and refrigerate several hours to blend flavours. Yields 2 cups.

Each tablespoon contains:

Calories	*14*	*Protein*	*1.5g*
Carbohydrates	*0.2g*	*Total fats*	*0.8g*
		(Saturated fat 0.1g)	

WHITMAN INN'S STUFFED SQUASH BLOSSOMS

WHITMAN INN

Nancy Gurnham has added a new dimension to her culinary artistry. She picks fully open squash blossoms and serves them stuffed with seasoned rice.

1 1/2 tablespoons butter
1/2 small onion, minced
1-2 garlic cloves, minced
1/2 cup long grain rice
1/4 cup wild rice
1/4 cup capellini or vermicelli pasta, broken in small pieces
1/2 cup chanterelle mushrooms, thinly sliced (may use cultivated white mushrooms)
1 1/4 cups chicken stock
1 1/2 teaspoons parsley, chopped
1/2 teaspoon dried basil
1/4 teaspoon dried thyme
1 1/2 teaspoons Worcestershire sauce
1/2 teaspoon Outerbridges Sherry Pepper Sauce (optional)
16-20 fully opened squash blossoms

Melt butter and sauté onion and garlic until softened. Add rices and pasta and sauté 5 minutes, stirring constantly, until golden. Stir in mushrooms, herbs and sauces. Add chicken broth, bring to a boil, reduce heat and simmer, covered, until rice is tender, approximately 20 minutes. Check during the last 5 minutes of cooking and add a little water if necessary. Set rice aside and cool.

Preheat oven to 350°F. Gently wash and dry blossoms. Gently fill each blossom with rice mixture, then fold petals over the open end to seal. Place blossoms on a greased baking sheet and spray lightly with Pam. Bake 15 to 20 minutes and serve immediately. Serves 4 to 6.

Each serving contains:

Calories	*95*	*Protein*	*3.2g*
Carbohydrates	*14.3g*	*Total fats*	*3.3g*
		(Saturated fat 1.9g)	

WHIPPED CREAM CHEESE SPREAD

BLUENOSE LODGE

Try this delightful spread on your morning bagel. By using light cream cheese and adding the low fat yoghurt you decrease the fat in the recipe without compromising the flavour. In testing this recipe, we added a few chopped pecans to one half and slivers of smoked salmon to the other. Voilà, instant canâpé spreads!

1 8-ounce package light cream cheese, at
   room temperature
1/3 cup plain low-fat yoghurt

Process the cream cheese in a food processor or with an electric mixer. Add yoghurt and process until blended. Yields 1 cup.

Each tablespoon contains:

Calories	*35*	*Protein*	*1.8g*
Carbohydrates	*1.4g*	*Total fats*	*2.5g*
		(Saturated fat 1.6g)	

BRUSCHETTA

SUNSHINE CAFÉ

You can almost smell the tantalizing Mediterranean aroma of this appetizer just by reading the recipe.

1 loaf French or Italian bread, sliced in half
   lengthwise, or Focaccia bread
1 1/2 cups tomato, skinned, seeded and diced
1/2 cup Mozzarella cheese, grated
1 tablespoon Parmesan cheese
1/4 cup extra virgin olive oil
1 tablespoon garlic, finely chopped
1 tablespoon basil, finely chopped (1 teaspoon
   dry)
2 teaspoons parsley, chopped
salt and black pepper, freshly ground, to taste

Preheat oven to 400°F. Prepare bread and place on baking sheet. (If using both halves of the French or Italian bread to make two bruschettas, then double the tomato/cheese mixture.) Mix remaining ingredients together and spread evenly over bread. Bake in preheated oven until browned and bubbly, approximately 8 to 10 minutes. Slice to serve. Serves 6.

Each serving contains:

Calories	*134*	*Protein*	*3.2g*
Carbohydrates	*4.4g*	*Total fats*	*11.9g*
		(Saturated fat 2.9g)	

BAY OF FUNDY MUSSELS IN A SPICY THAI SAUCE

PASAMAQUODDY DINING ROOM AT THE ALGONQUIN HOTEL

If you enjoy freshly steamed Atlantic mussels then you will have to try this creation from the chefs at the Algonquin Hotel. They have combined this delicate crustacean with a spicy oriental Thai sauce and have created a truly exotic appetizer. The fish sauce, known as Nam Pla, is available in oriental specialty shops.

3-4 pounds fresh mussels
1 tablespoon fresh ginger, minced
1 tablespoon garlic, minced
2 tablespoons fresh cilantro (coriander), chopped
2 tablespoons fresh basil, chopped
1 stalk fresh lemongrass, chopped (if unavailable, substitute 1 teaspoon lemon zest)
4 green onions, chopped
pinch of dried red chili flakes
1 tablespoon fish sauce
2 tablespoons Hoisin sauce
1 tablespoon soy sauce
1 tablespoon fresh lime juice
1/4 cup orange juice
zest of 1 lime
15 black peppercorns, crushed
2/3 cup coconut milk

Wash and remove beards from the mussels, discarding any that are open or have broken shells. Combine remaining ingredients in a large stockpot and stir to mix well. Bring sauce to a boil and immediately add mussels. Cover and steam mussels until they open, approximately 5 to 7 minutes. Discard any mussels that did not open.

To serve, portion mussels in serving bowls and ladle sauce over them. Garnish with additional sprigs of fresh cilantro. Serves 4 to 6.

Each serving contains:

Calories	230	*Protein*	13.7g
Carbohydrates	27.1g	*Total fats*	10.0g
			(Saturated fat 6.5g)

LUNENBURG STEAMED MUSSELS

THE COMPASS ROSE INN

When we visit the seashore we expect the freshest of seafood. At the Compass Rose Inn our expectations are always fulfilled!

4 pounds mussels
2/3 cup white wine
2/3 cup water
2 teaspoons lemon juice
1/2 teaspoon pepper, freshly ground
1/2 teaspoon garlic powder
2/3 cup celery, chopped
2/3 cup green onion, minced

Scrub mussels thoroughly, discarding any that are open and will not close when lightly tapped. Place in a large kettle on a steamer rack, add wine, water, lemon juice, pepper and garlic, and sprinkle with celery and green onions. Cover and bring to a boil. Steam 8 minutes. When shells have opened, pile mussels in heated serving bowls, discarding any that are not open. Spoon broth over mussels. Serves 3 to 4.

Each serving contains:

Calories	133	*Protein*	14.0g
Carbohydrates	6.9g	*Total fats*	2.6g
			(Saturated fat 1.0g)

Bay of Fundy Mussels in Spicy Thai Sauce ▶

DANFORTH AVENUE HUMMUS DIP

INN ON THE COVE

Innkeepers Willa and Ross Mavis spent several years living in Toronto, enjoying the delightful variety of ethnic foods available in the various parts of the city. They frequently prepare this Hummus Dip, which they serve with toasted pita bread triangles.

1 can chick peas (19 ounces)
4 large cloves garlic, peeled
1/4 cup tahini (sesame seed paste)
1 teaspoon lemon juice
1/4 cup olive oil
salt and pepper, to taste
1/4 teaspoon cayenne pepper
fresh parsley, for garnish

Drain chick peas and reserve liquid. In a food processor finely chop garlic and chick peas. Add tahini, olive oil and lemon juice and process until smooth. To make dip less thick and more creamy, slowly add chick pea liquid until desired consistency is reached. Season with salt and pepper. Serve dip in a decorative bowl sprinkled with a dusting of cayenne pepper and chopped parsley. Yields 2 1/2 cups.

Each tablespoon contains:

Calories	*35*	*Protein*	*1.0g*
Carbohydrates	*2.8g*	*Total fats*	*2.4g*
		(Saturated fat 0.3g)	

ACTON'S SMOKED SALMON PÂTÉ

ACTON'S GRILL & CAFÉ

The flavour of smoked salmon is unbeatable but unfortunately the price is usually high. As this recipe uses a small amount of salmon, you can still treat your guests while keeping the cost reasonable.

8 ounces smoked salmon
1/2 cup cream cheese or light cream cheese
1/4 cup unsalted butter
1 tablespoon fresh dill, chopped
pinch of dry mustard

Place salmon in bowl of food processor and process with on/off motion until finely ground. Cut cream cheese and butter into cubes, add to salmon and process until well mixed. Add dill and dry mustard and process until creamy.

Smooth pâté into serving dish, garnish with additional sprigs of fresh dill, cover and refrigerate. Serve with assorted crackers. Yields approximately 1 cup.

Each tablespoon contains:

Calories	*60*	*Protein*	*3.4g*
Carbohydrates	*0.6g*	*Total fats*	*4.9g*
		(Saturated fat 2.8g)	

Acton's Smoked Salmon Pâté ▶

PROSCIUTTO ON MANGO

LITTLE SHEMOGUE COUNTRY INN

The mango: what a glorious fruit! The flavour is exotic and the versatile fruit lends itself to a variety of dishes ranging from appetizers to main entrées and desserts.

2 tablespoons olive oil
4 tablespoons sunflower oil
zest from 2 limes
2 tablespoons gingerroot, freshly grated
2 tablespoons fresh lime juice
1 large ripe mango
12 slices prosciutto ham, thinly sliced

Whisk together the oils, lime zest, gingerroot and lime juice until the vinaigrette is emulsified. Peel the mango and cut in medium strips. Arrange the mango strips and prosciutto attractively on serving dishes. Drizzle with vinaigrette and serve immediately. Serves 4.

Each serving contains:

Calories	*259*	*Protein*	*6.3g*
Carbohydrates	*10.5g*	*Total fats*	*22.2g*
		(Saturated fat 2.9g)	

POTATO CRISPS WITH SOUR CREAM & CAVIAR

THE PINES RESORT HOTEL

The chefs at the Pines find that these tasty little potato appetizers lend themselves to a variety of toppings. Instead of caviar you may want to try sour cream and smoked salmon, sour cream and apple sauce, olive paste or a dab of anchovy paste.

3 baking potatoes, peeled
1/4 cup fresh chives, chopped
1/4 cup parsley, chopped
salt
pepper, freshly ground, to taste
vegetable oil for frying
1/2 cup sour cream or light sour cream
2 ounces salmon caviar
1/4 cup fresh chives, chopped (2nd amount)

Grate potatoes with a hand grater or the grating attachment of your food processor. Combine grated potatoes, chives, parsley, salt and pepper in a bowl.

In a large skillet, heat a film of oil on high heat. For each crisp, drop 1 tablespoon of potato mixture onto skillet and flatten with a spatula. Fry until golden, about 2 minutes. Flip crisps and cook until browned. Drain crisps on paper towel and reserve. Repeat process until all mixture is used.

Serve crisps cold, or reheat in a preheated 375°F oven for 5 minutes. Top with sour cream, caviar and a sprinkling of chives. Serves 4.

Each serving contains:

Calories	*184*	*Protein*	*16.9g*
Carbohydrates	*18.5g*	*Total fats*	*10.2g*
		(Saturated fat 1.4g)	

Prosciutto on Mango ▶

SMOKED SALMON BRIE WHEEL

HADDON HALL

This appetizer is simply a cook's delight. It is easy to make, can be prepared in advance and tastes wonderful.

6 ounces smoked salmon, finely chopped
2 Brie cheese wheels, 125 grams each
fresh dill, finely chopped

Cut each Brie cheese into 3 even rounds. An easy way to do this is to use a length of fine dental floss. Wrap the floss around the cheese, cross the ends of the floss and pull to evenly slice; repeat.

Layer smoked salmon on the two inside slices of each Brie. Completely cover the outside of each cheese with finely chopped dill and press to adhere. Wrap wheels in plastic wrap and seal tightly. Refrigerate for 24 hours. Cut in wedges with a sharp knife and serve as an *hors d'oeuvre* or starter to a seafood meal. Yields 2 wheels.

Each Brie wheel contains:

Calories	*485*	*Protein*	*39.7g*
Carbohydrates	*2.2g*	*Total fats*	*35.2g*
			(Saturated fat 20.5g)

SUN–DRIED TOMATO DIP WITH CRUDITÉS

KELTIC LODGE

The chefs at Keltic Lodge use sun-dried tomatoes in this easy-to-prepare vegetable dip, capturing the colour and pungent flavour of Italian plum tomatoes. Their use of low-fat dairy products makes it healthy too.

2-3 cloves garlic, crushed
1/4 teaspoon salt
6-8 sun-dried tomatoes, softened
1 cup non-fat cottage cheese
1/3 cup non-fat plain yoghurt
1/4 cup low-fat mayonnaise
fresh chives, chopped
assorted dipping vegetables, cut in bite-sized
    pieces (broccoli, mushrooms, green and red
    peppers, cucumbers, carrot sticks etc.)

Combine garlic, salt and tomatoes in a food processor and process until mixture becomes a coarse paste. Add cottage cheese, yoghurt and mayonnaise and blend until smooth. Turn dip into decorative dish, garnish with chives, and place in centre of a platter. Arrange assorted vegetables in an attractive fashion around dip. Yields 1 3/4 cups.

Each tablespoon contains:

Calories	*39*	*Protein*	*2.8g*
Carbohydrates	*7.2g*	*Total fats*	*0.5g*
			(Saturated fat 0.2g)

Smoked Salmon Brie Wheel ▶

SOUPS

Once again we challenged our Maritime chefs to provide recipes for new and healthy soups, and we have not been disappointed. In fact, we continue to be surprised by their ingenuity as they marry local products with herbs, spices and a variety of ingredients.

For those sunny summer days we suggest you try the Chilled Red Plum Soup from Cooper's Inn & Restaurant. When the weather turns, try the elegant Squash Soup with Pernod Swirl from White Point Beach Lodge.

◀ *Mussel Soup*

MUSSEL SOUP

THE LION INN

At The Lion Inn, the richness of this delicious seafood soup comes from the addition of heavy cream. A lighter version can be achieved by using blend (12% m.f.), milk or a combination of both.

2-3 pounds mussels
5 cups water
1 1/2-2 cups white wine
2 celery stalks, finely chopped
2 medium onions, finely chopped
1 medium carrot, finely chopped
2 cloves garlic, cut in half
3 bay leaves
1 tablespoon dried parsley
1/2 teaspoon dried basil
1/4 teaspoon dried tarragon
1 lemon wedge
heavy cream (35% m.f.)

Scrub and debeard the mussels, being careful to discard any that are open or have broken shells.

In a large pot, add water, white wine and all ingredients except the mussels. Bring to a boil and simmer for 2 minutes. Add mussels and cook at medium-high heat until the mussels open, approximately 4 to 5 minutes. Remove mussels from soup and reserve.

Pour stock into a large bowl and discard the garlic, lemon and bay leaves. When mussels are cool enough to handle, remove the meat and add to the stock. Stock may be refrigerated up to 1 week.

To serve, heat stock, stir in cream to taste and serve with a garnish of fresh parsley. Serves 6.

Each serving contains:
Calories	*127*	*Protein*	*7.1g*
Carbohydrates	*7.9g*	*Total fats*	*3.6g*
		(Saturated fat 1.7g)	

ZUCCHINI & LEEK SOUP WITH FRESH BASIL

DUNCREIGAN COUNTRY INN

Eleanor Mullendore prepares this colourful soup when garden vegetables are at their prime. She serves it with a swirl of pesto and herbed crostini.

1 large leek, cleaned and roughly chopped
2-3 cloves garlic, minced
1 tablespoon olive oil
3 cups chicken broth
1/4 cup dry white wine
1 large potato, peeled and chopped
3 large sprigs of parsley, chopped
2 bay leaves
4 medium zucchini, chopped
1 cup fresh basil leaves
1/2 cup heavy cream or mixture of cream and milk
salt and pepper, to taste
pesto (see recipe, page 61), for garnish
parmesan cheese, grated, and crostini (croutons), for garnish

Remove the green top of the leek and rinse white part thoroughly, removing any grit; roughly chop. Sauté leek with garlic in olive oil until vegetables are wilted. Add chicken broth, wine, potato chunks, parsley and bay leaves. Bring to a simmer, cover and cook 10 minutes. Add chopped zucchini and continue cooking until vegetables are tender. Remove bay leaves and transfer to a food processor. Purée in batches. Strain the purée through a fine sieve or food mill.

In a clean food processor bowl, purée basil leaves with 1 tablespoon water. Return puréed stock to a heavy pot, add basil purée and reheat. Stir in cream and season with salt and pepper. Ladle into soup bowls, swirl with a teaspoon of pesto, if desired, and top with grated parmesan cheese and crostini. Serves 4.

Each serving contains:
Calories	*267*	*Protein*	*15.0g*
Carbohydrates	*22.9g*	*Total fats*	*14.1g*
		(Saturated fat 5.2g)	

EGG DROP SOUP

QUACO INN

Betty Ann Murray of Quaco Inn developed this recipe and triples it to serve twelve. For those concerned about cholesterol, she tells us that "egg beaters" can be substituted for the whole eggs.

4 cups rich chicken broth
2 tablespoons cornstarch
1/4 cup cold water
4-5 small mushrooms, thinly sliced
2 small green onions, sliced
2-3 stalks celery, sliced
1/2 cup frozen peas
1 egg

Bring broth to a boil over medium-high heat. Stir in cornstarch that has been dissolved in 1/4 cup cold water. Return to a boil and simmer 10 minutes, until broth has thickened slightly. Add mushrooms, green onions, celery and peas. Bring back to a hard boil, and cook until vegetables are slightly tender. In a small bowl, whisk egg and then pour in a thin stream into the boiling soup while stirring with a fork. Serve immediately. Serves 4.

Each serving contains:

Calories	*120*	*Protein*	*9.5g*
Carbohydrates	*14.7g*	*Total fats*	*3.0g*
		(Saturated fat 0.8g)	

POTATO SOUP WITH CURRY & RED OR OAK-LEAF LETTUCE

THE AMHERST SHORE
COUNTRY INN

Owner and chef Donna Laceby tells us this award winning soup is best if made a day ahead, cooled and refrigerated. For a lighter soup, she suggests replacing the cream with blend or milk.

1/4 cup butter
1 1/2 cups Spanish onions, chopped medium
   fine
8 small potatoes, peeled and sliced
2 cups rich chicken stock
1-1 1/2 teaspoons curry powder
salt and pepper, to taste
2 cups heavy cream
3 ounces red or oak-leaf lettuce or spinach,
   washed and sliced

Melt butter in a large saucepan over medium heat. Sauté onions and potatoes 3 to 4 minutes, stirring occasionally. Add stock and 1 teaspoon of curry, simmer until potatoes are tender, approximately 20 minutes. Add cream, reheat to boiling, adjust flavouring by adding more curry, if desired. Season with salt and pepper. Cool, then refrigerate overnight. At serving time, bring soup to a boil, stir in lettuce or spinach and serve. Serves 6.

Each serving (when tested with milk) contains:

Calories	*192*	*Protein*	*6.0g*
Carbohydrates	*24.7g*	*Total fats*	*8.3g*
		(Saturated fat 4.9g)	

ROASTED FENNEL BROTH WITH NEW BRUNSWICK FIDDLEHEADS

PASAMAQUODDY DINING ROOM AT THE ALGONQUIN HOTEL

The spring gathering of fiddleheads is a cherished New Brunswick tradition. The chefs at the Algonquin Hotel honour this unique New Brunswick vegetable in a delightfully different soup.

4 fresh fennel bulbs, trimmed
2 medium onions, chopped
2 medium carrots, chopped
4 celery stalks, chopped
1 leek, cleaned and chopped
4 cloves garlic, chopped
2 tablespoons fennel seed
4 litres water
1 teaspoon salt
20 whole black peppercorns
3 bay leaves
1 pound fresh fiddleheads, cleaned and
    trimmed
2 ounces Pernod liqueur
fennel sprigs, for garnish

Preheat oven to 400°F. Place fennel bulbs on a baking sheet and roast in oven until tender and golden brown, approximately 20 to 25 minutes. Remove from oven and roughly chop.

In a large stockpot, combine chopped fennel, onion, carrot, celery, leek, garlic and fennel seed. Cover with water and bring to a boil. Add salt, peppercorns and bay leaves, reduce heat, and simmer uncovered, until liquid is reduced by 1/2, approximately 1 1/2 to 2 hours.

Strain broth, return to stockpot and reheat. Add fiddleheads and Pernod and simmer until fiddleheads are just tender. Adjust seasoning to taste. Serve immediately in warm bowls garnished with fennel sprigs. Serves 6.

Each serving contains:

Calories	193	*Protein*	6.2g
Carbohydrates	40.6g	*Total fats*	1.7g
		(Saturated fat 0.3g)	

SQUASH SOUP WITH PERNOD SWIRL

WHITE POINT BEACH LODGE

With its dash of Pernod liqueur, this hearty soup developed by chef Chris Profit is both simple to prepare and elegant.

1 cup onions, peeled and diced
3 tablespoons vegetable oil
1 teaspoon cinnamon
1 teaspoon ground cumin
pinch cayenne
3 tablespoons brown sugar
8 cups squash, peeled and cubed
6 cups chicken broth
1/4 cup lemon juice
1/4 cup white wine
salt and pepper, to taste
1/2 cup light sour cream
2 tablespoons Pernod liqueur

Sauté onions in vegetable oil until light brown. Add cinnamon, cumin and cayenne and cook 3 to 5 minutes, stirring frequently. Add sugar, squash, stock, lemon juice and wine. Cover, bring to a boil over medium heat and simmer until vegetables are cooked, approximately 35 minutes. Strain liquid into a large bowl and reserve.

Purée vegetables in a food processor until smooth. Add to reserved liquid and adjust seasoning with salt and pepper. Return to medium heat and simmer 10 to 15 minutes. In a small bowl, whisk together sour cream and Pernod. To serve, ladle soup into bowls, top with 1 1/2 teaspoons of sour cream mixture and swirl with a spoon. Serves 6 to 8.

Each serving contains:

Calories	161	*Protein*	5.9g
Carbohydrates	17.7g	*Total fats*	6.8g
		(Saturated fat 0.9g)	

Roasted Fennel Broth ▶

CHILLED RED PLUM SOUP

COOPER'S INN & RESTAURANT

Allan Redmond of the Cooper's Inn tells us that this soup, with its hint of pure Nova Scotia maple syrup, is a favourite with guests on warm summer evenings.

1 large slice fresh ginger, peeled
1/2 cinnamon stick
1/4 teaspoon allspice
3-4 black peppercorns
2 1/2 pounds very ripe red plums, pitted and
    chopped
3 cups apple juice
1/2 cup maple syrup (or to taste)
1 tablespoon fresh lemon juice (or to taste)
low-fat sour cream
toasted and sliced almonds

Make a *sachet d'épices* (spice sack) by placing ginger, cinnamon, allspice and peppercorns in a small cheesecloth bag. In a medium pot combine *sachet d'épices*, plums, and apple juice. Simmer until plums are soft. Remove *sachet d'épices*. Pour into a food processor and purée. Strain the purée through a sieve. Add maple syrup and lemon juice to taste. Chill and serve with a dollop of sour cream and a sprinkling of toasted almonds. Serves 4.

Each serving contains:

Calories	*377*	*Protein*	*3.4g*
Carbohydrates	*86.7g*	*Total fats*	*4.5g*
		(Saturated fat 0.4g)	

LEEK & STILTON SOUP

ACTON'S GRILL & CAFÉ

You will always find innovative soups on the menu of this cheery restaurant. We feel certain that this soup, with its marvellous blend of nutmeg, dill and Stilton, will become a favourite.

3 small or 2 medium leeks
1/4 cup butter
2 large onions, diced
1 tablespoon Dijon mustard
4 cups chicken stock
pinch of nutmeg
white pepper, to taste
1/2 teaspoon dried dillweed
4 cups potato, peeled and cut in half-inch
    cubes
1 cup blend (12% m.f.)
1/4 cup fresh dill, chopped
4 ounces Stilton cheese, crumbled (makes
    approximately 1 cup)

Prepare leeks by cutting off tough green sections, washing well to remove grit and slicing into 1/2-inch pieces. Melt butter in a heavy-bottomed saucepan, add leeks and onions and sauté until soft. Add Dijon mustard, stock, nutmeg, pepper and dillweed; cover and bring to a boil. Add potatoes, reduce heat and simmer, stirring often, until potatoes are soft, approximately 25 minutes.

In a food processor, purée soup in batches until smooth. Return soup to saucepan, add blend and dill and gently reheat being careful not to boil. Serve topped with crumbled Stilton cheese. Serves 6.

Each serving contains:

Calories	*293*	*Protein*	*11.2g*
Carbohydrates	*21g*	*Total fats*	*19g*
		(Saturated fat 11.5g)	

Leek & Stilton Soup ▶

TOMATO & FENNEL SOUP WITH STEAMED MUSSELS

UNNI'S

This is a hearty soup, suitable for an appetizer or, when served with a salad and crusty bread, as a luncheon entrée.

1 tablespoon whole fennel seed
2 green onions, chopped
1 yellow onion, julienned
6 cloves garlic, chopped
1 tablespoon vegetable oil
1 tablespoon instant seafood or vegetable stock base
18 ounces tinned tomatoes, crushed with juice
2 1/4 cups cold water
3 pounds cultivated mussels
1 sprig parsley, chopped
salt and pepper, to taste

In a large saucepan, sauté fennel seeds, green and yellow onions and garlic in oil until softened. Stir stock base into fennel mixture and add tomatoes and water. Bring to a boil, reduce heat and simmer 20 minutes.

While tomatoes are cooking, scrub and debeard mussels. Steam mussels in a small amount of water until fully opened, about 5 minutes. Discard any mussels that do not open.

Add parsley to soup, season with salt and pepper and simmer 3 additional minutes. To serve, divide mussels amongst serving bowls and cover with soup. Serves 4 to 6.

Each serving contains:
Calories   163   Protein   13.7g
Carbohydrates   18.7g   Total fats   5.1g
*   (Saturated fat 0.7g)*

WATERCRESS SOUP

THE DUNES CAFÉ

At The Dunes, chef Heiko Weirich garnishes this delicate soup with squid ink pasta for an interesting contrast in colour.

1/2 cup butter
2 shallots, minced
1/3 cup white wine
5 cups blend (12% m.f.) or milk (also successfully tested using 1 1/2 cups blend and 3 1/2 cups milk)
2 bayleaves, broken in large pieces
20 white peppercorns
1 large bunch watercress, finely chopped
seasalt, to taste
1/3 cup heavy cream (35% m.f.)

Melt butter in a heavy-bottomed saucepan. Add shallots and sauté until softened. Add wine and stir to deglaze the pot. Stir in blend or milk, bayleaf and peppercorns. Simmer for 15 minutes, stirring occasionally and being careful not to boil. Pour liquid through a fine mesh strainer to remove small bits. Return to saucepan, add watercress and simmer for another 5 minutes. Add seasalt to taste, stir in cream and serve immediately. Serves 4.

Each serving contains:
Calories   599   Protein   15.0g
Carbohydrates   40.8g   Total fats   44.7g
*   (Saturated fat 27.4g)*

Tomato & Fennel Soup with Mussels ▶

ANNAPOLIS VALLEY APPLE BROTH WITH GOAT CHEESE FRITTERS

THE INN AT BAY FORTUNE

We were delighted to find a recipe featuring our Annapolis Valley apples. Chef Michael Smith prepares this delightful broth and serves it topped with cheese fritters.

1 large onion, sliced
1 carrot, diced
1/4 cup olive oil
1 large clove garlic, minced
6 Cortland apples, cored and roughly chopped
6 cups apple cider
1 bay leaf
3 cups apple wine
salt and pepper, to taste

In a large kettle over medium heat, sweat onion and carrot in oil over medium heat until caramelized. Add garlic and sweat an additional minute. Stir in prepared apples, cider, bay leaf and wine. Bring to a simmer and reduce by 1/3. Purée in a blender, in batches, and strain through a fine mesh strainer. Season to taste with salt and pepper and return to serving temperature. Serve in individual bowls topped with 1 or 2 fritters. Serves 6.

Each serving contains:

Calories	369	*Protein*	0.9g
Carbohydrates	53.6g	*Total fats*	9.9g
		(Saturated fat 1.4g)	

Goat Cheese Fritters:

1/2 cup water
1/4 cup butter
1/2 cup all purpose flour
1/2 teaspoon baking powder
1/2 teaspoon nutmeg
1/4 teaspoon salt
1/4 teaspoon pepper
2 eggs
4 ounces Chevre cheese
extra virgin olive oil

In a medium-sized saucepan, bring water and butter to a rolling boil over medium-high heat. Sift together the dry ingredients and add all at once to the boiling water. Stir vigorously with a wooden spoon until a smooth dough is formed. Remove from heat.

Thoroughly combine the eggs and cheese in a food processor. Place dough in a mixer with paddle running at low speed. Slowly add egg mixture and beat until completely combined. Pour enough olive oil into a frying pan to barely cover the bottom. Heat to 350°F and, using 2 teaspoons, form dough into small balls, drop into pan and fry, turning once until golden and puffy, approximately 3 to 4 minutes. Drain on paper towelling and serve immediately. Yields 12 fritters.

Two fritters contain:

Calories	231	*Protein*	7.0g
Carbohydrates	8.6g	*Total fats*	19.0g
		(Saturated fat 10.0g)	

Annapolis Valley Apple Broth with Goat Cheese Fritters ▶

SALADS

*I*t is easy to experiment with a salad. Toss a variety of greens with a vinaigrette and serve as one course of a dinner; or add meats or seafood to make the salad a meal in itself. The salads featured here are unique and innovative with something for even the most discriminating palate.

For lighter fare, you may want to try try the oil-free Green Salad with Raspberry Vinaigrette from Cooper's Inn & Restaurant or the Low Cal Caesar Salad from Steamers Stop Inn. For adventure, try the Tabbouleh Salad from Haddon Hall or the Fennel and Grapefruit Salad from Halliburton House Inn.

◄ *Grapefruit & Fennel Salad with Sun-dried Tomato Vinaigrette*

GRAPEFRUIT & FENNEL SALAD WITH SUN-DRIED TOMATO VINAIGRETTE

HALLIBURTON HOUSE INN

The aromatic licorice flavour of fennel accents this unique salad. The chef suggests that the amount of fennel you use will depend upon personal preference.

2 large or 3 medium grapefruit
mixed greens (raddichio, chicory, endive, oakleaf, romaine etc.), to serve 6
fresh fennel bulb
toasted sesame seeds, for garnish
Sun-dried Tomato Vinaigrette (recipe follows)

Peel and section grapefruit, removing pith and seeds. Divide greens between 6 serving plates and top with grapefruit sections and 3 to 6 slivers of fennel. Drizzle with vinaigrette and garnish with toasted sesame seeds. Serves 6.

Sun-dried Tomato Vinaigrette:

5 sun-dried tomato pieces
1 1/2 tablespoons balsamic vinegar
1 1/2 tablespoons red wine vinegar
1 large clove garlic, minced with dash of salt
2/3 cup olive oil
1 teaspoon fresh basil (or 1/4 teaspoon dried)

Reconstitute sun-dried tomatoes with a little olive oil until softened. In a food processor, purée tomatoes, vinegars and garlic. Slowly add olive oil in a steady stream until emulsified. Stir in basil. Yields 1 cup.

Each serving contains:

Calories	189	Protein	5.8g
Carbohydrates	22.4g	Total fats	10.7g
		(Saturated fat 1.4g)	

WARM RED CABBAGE SALAD

CHARLOTTE LANE CAFÉ & CRAFTS

Those who think that a salad must be well chilled and crunchy are in for a pleasant surprise with Roland Glauser's warm cabbage version. The colour, aroma and taste of this salad elevate the lowly cabbage to a new high in cuisine.

1 small red cabbage, cored and finely sliced
2 cloves garlic, finely chopped
6 slices crisp bacon
1/4 cup balsamic vinegar
1/3 cup virgin olive oil
2/3 cup Parmesan cheese
lettuce
fresh basil
black pepper, freshly ground

Sauté cabbage, garlic and bacon in vinegar and oil until the cabbage is slightly softened. Add Parmesan cheese and toss to coat. Serve immediately on a bed of lettuce leaves garnished with fresh basil and a grating of ground pepper. Serves 4.

Each serving contains:

Calories	364	Protein	13.5g
Carbohydrates	20.6g	Total fats	27.7g
		(Saturated fat 6.8g)	

LOW-CAL CAESAR SALAD

STEAMERS STOP INN

Pat Stewart of Steamers Stop Inn tells us that this salad dressing will keep in the refrigerator for up to three weeks. If you are a Caesar Salad advocate, we suggest doubling the dressing recipe!

2 large heads romaine lettuce
1-2 cloves garlic (or to taste)
2 tablespoons low-fat plain yoghurt
1 teaspoon dry mustard
2 tablespoons cider vinegar
2 tablespoons lemon juice
1/4 teaspoon salt
1/4 teaspoon pepper
2 teaspoons sugar
1 teaspoon Dijon mustard
1/2 cup corn oil
1/2 cup grated Parmesan cheese
croutons

Wash and dry lettuce, tear into bite-sized pieces and place in a salad bowl. Place garlic cloves, yoghurt and dry mustard in a blender and process 1 minute. Add the vinegar, lemon juice, salt, pepper, sugar and Dijon mustard and process an additional minute. Continue blending and add oil in a slow stream. Process until emulsified, approximately 2 minutes.

Toss lettuce with dressing; top with Parmesan cheese and croutons. Serves 8 to10.

Each serving contains:
Calories	*123*	*Protein*	*3.3g*
Carbohydrates	*4.7g*	*Total fats*	*10.5g*
		(Saturated fat 1.8g)	

ASSORTED GREENS WITH POPPY SEED DRESSING

THE PALLISER

This vinaigrette-style dressing is sweet yet tangy and is a nice accompaniment to assorted greens of the season. It is quick to prepare and stores well in the refrigerator.

combination of salad greens (romaine, iceberg, oak leaf etc.), torn in bite-sized pieces, to serve 6
tomato, cut in wedges
cucumber, sliced
red and/or green pepper, julienned

Arrange salad ingredients in a large salad bowl. Drizzle with Poppy Seed Dressing and gently toss to coat. Serve immediately. Serves 6.

Poppy Seed Dressing:

1 tablespoon onion, finely diced
2 tablespoons sugar
1/4 teaspoon salt
3/4 teaspoon dry mustard
1/3 cup cider vinegar
2/3 cup vegetable oil
2 teaspoons poppy seeds

Purée onion, sugar, salt and dry mustard in a food processor, then add cider vinegar. Continue processing, adding oil in a slow stream until emulsified. Stir in poppy seeds. Yields 1 cup.

Each serving contains:
Calories	*131*	*Protein*	*3.7g*
Carbohydrates	*9.6g*	*Total fats*	*10.1g*
		(Saturated fat 1.1g)	

ACTON'S GREEK SALAD

ACTON'S GRILL & CAFÉ

Be sure to allow the tomatoes and onions in this salad to marinate for an hour.
The result is well worth the time spent preparing this delicious dish.

3 tablespoons red wine vinegar
3 garlic cloves, crushed
1/2 teaspoon sugar
1 teaspoon oregano
1/4 teaspoon salt
1/4 teaspoon pepper, freshly ground
1/4 teaspoon cayenne pepper
1 teaspoon anchovy paste (optional)
1/3 cup olive oil
4 large tomatoes, seeded and chopped in bite-size pieces
1 small red onion, finely sliced
10 cups mixed salad greens (romaine, leaf, escarole, arugula etc.)
2 green onions, thinly sliced
1/3 cup small black olives
1/4 cup fresh mint leaves, chopped
1 sweet green pepper, cut in chunks
1/2 English cucumber, cut in chunks
1 cup feta cheese, crumbled

In a medium-size bowl, whisk together vinegar, garlic, sugar, oregano, salt, pepper, cayenne and anchovy paste. Slowly beat in oil until emulsified. Stir tomatoes and red onion into dressing and let stand, uncovered, at room temperature for 1 or more hours. Stir occasionally.

In a large salad bowl, toss together greens, green onion, olives, mint, green pepper and cucumber. Pour marinated tomato mixture over greens and toss. Sprinkle with feta cheese and serve immediately. Serves 6.

Each serving contains:

Calories	*246*	*Protein*	*7.9g*
Carbohydrates	*18.4g*	*Total fats*	*17.6g*
		(Saturated fat 4.7g)	

Acton's Greek Salad ▶

TOMATO BASIL SALAD

THE PINES RESORT HOTEL

This is a colourful little salad that can be prepared quickly. It is ideal for the cook who has access to an herb garden.

3-4 plum tomatoes
16 slices fresh buffalo mozzarella cheese
  (boconccini)
salt, to taste
pepper, freshly ground, to taste
3 tablespoons extra virgin olive oil
3/4 teaspoon fresh Greek oregano, chopped
12 purple basil leaves

Slice tomatoes 1/4 inch thick, discarding stem ends. Cut cheese slices into rounds, approximately the same size as tomato slices. Arrange 4 slices of tomato and cheese on 4 serving plates, alternating in order and slightly overlapping. Sprinkle with salt and freshly ground pepper. Drizzle with olive oil and sprinkle with oregano. Garnish with basil leaves. Serves 4.

Each serving contains:
Calories	*206*	*Protein*	*7.2g*
Carbohydrates	*6.6g*	*Total fats*	*17.6g*
		(Saturated fat 5.9g)	

FRESH MUSHROOMS & ARTICHOKES, GREEK STYLE

CHEZ FRANÇOISE

The ancient Greeks so honoured basil that they served it only to their rulers. Today's chefs use it as a flavouring for Greek, southern French and Italian cuisines.

1/2 pound fresh mushrooms, cleaned and
  sliced
1 19-ounce can artichoke hearts
3/4 cup olive oil
1/2 cup lemon juice
1 tablespoon sugar
2 teaspoons dry mustard
1/2 tablespoon fresh basil, chopped, or 1/2
  teaspoon dried basil
1 clove garlic, crushed and finely chopped
1 tablespoon sweet red pepper, finely chopped
salt and pepper, to taste
Bibb lettuce, to serve 4
fresh mint leaves, for garnish

Prepare mushrooms; drain and quarter artichoke hearts. Whisk together olive oil, lemon juice, sugar, mustard, basil, garlic and red pepper. Season with salt and pepper. Marinate mushrooms and artichokes several hours. To serve, arrange Bibb lettuce on 4 serving plates, divide mushrooms and artichokes between plates and drizzle with vinaigrette. Garnish with mint leaves. Serves 4.

Each serving contains:
Calories	*206*	*Protein*	*5.8g*
Carbohydrates	*19.2g*	*Total fats*	*14.1g*
		(Saturated fat 1.9g)	

ROASTED ONION, ENDIVE & ORANGE SALAD

THE PINES RESORT HOTEL

The chef tells us that you can omit the step of roasting the onion, but we feel roasting brings out a sweetness that complements the orange and contrasts with the watercress and endive.

4 red onions, cut into 8 wedges
1 tablespoon extra virgin olive oil
1 tablespoon balsamic vinegar
salt and pepper, to taste
1 bunch watercress, stalks removed
4 Belgian endives, in 1/2-inch slices
4 cups spinach, washed, dried and torn into
   bite-sized pieces
4 navel oranges
Lemon Vinaigrette (recipe follows)

Preheat oven to 400°F. Cut onion into wedges and toss with olive oil and balsamic vinegar. Season with salt and pepper and place on a cookie sheet. Bake until onion wedges are tender and browned, approximately 20 minutes. Reserve in a salad bowl.

Toss watercress leaves with onions. Add endive slices and spinach. Cut skin and white pith from oranges. Over a bowl, cut oranges into segments, reserving any juice that escapes. At serving time, combine orange slices, salad greens and onions. Drizzle with Lemon Vinaigrette and gently toss. Serves 4.

Lemon Vinaigrette:

1/4 cup fresh lemon juice
3 tablespoons orange juice, reserved
1 tablespoon white wine vinegar
1 tablespoon Dijon mustard
1/2 cup olive oil
salt and pepper, to taste

Combine lemon and orange juices. Add vinegar and Dijon mustard, and whisk in olive oil. Season with salt and pepper. Yields 3/4 cup.

Each serving contains:

Calories	*316*	*Protein*	*11.4g*
Carbohydrates	*49.5g*	*Total fats*	*11.8g*
		(Saturated fat 1.7g)	

THE LION INN HERITAGE SALAD

THE LION INN

George Morin, owner and chef at The Lion Inn, uses red wine vinegar to create his own variation of the popular Honey Mustard Salad Dressing. Its sweet and tangy flavour is simply delicious.

leaf lettuce, preferably red-top variety, to
    serve 6
2 ounces Stilton cheese, crumbled
watercress
1/3 cup walnuts, chopped

Prepare lettuce by washing, drying and breaking into bite-sized pieces. Arrange lettuce on individual serving dishes and top with watercress, cheese and walnuts. Drizzle with salad dressing and serve immediately. Serves 6.

Dressing:

1/4 cup red wine vinegar
1 cup olive oil
2 tablespoons honey
2 tablespoons Dijon mustard
salt and black pepper, to taste

Pour vinegar in a small bowl. With a wire whisk, gradually beat in olive oil until smooth. Beat in honey and mustard until emulsified. Add salt and pepper to taste. Store in a covered glass jar in refrigerator. Bring to room temperature before serving. Yields 1 1/4 cups.

Each serving contains:

Calories	190	Protein	2.8g
Carbohydrates	4.9g	Total fats	17.7g
		(Saturated fat 3.5g)	

STEAMED CHICKEN & SHRIMP SALAD

CHEZ LA VIGNE

With its garnish of bright edible flowers, this is a most attractive salad. In summer, chef Don Mailman uses red chili flowers but cautions that they are "hot." If you use them, remember to omit the banana or jalapeno peppers.

romaine lettuce leaves, to serve 6
1/2 English cucumber, sliced very thin
24 shrimp, peeled and deveined
3/4 pound cooked chicken, cubed
green onion, thinly sliced
1 grapefruit, peeled, white pith removed, and
    sectioned
1 tablespoon banana or jalapeno pepper,
    chopped
coriander sprigs
small edible flowers (pansy, violet, nasturtium
    etc.), for garnish

In a large salad bowl, toss lettuce, cucumber, shrimp and chicken. Arrange lettuce mixture on 6 individual salad plates, top with green onion, grapefruit sections, peppers, coriander and edible flowers. Drizzle vinaigrette over salad and serve immediately. Serves 6.

Vinaigrette:

1/3 cup olive oil
2 tablespoons lemon juice
2 tablespoons red wine vinegar
1 1/2 tablespoons soya sauce
2 tablespoons cranberry juice
1/2 teaspoon basil
salt and pepper, to taste

Process all ingredients, except oil, in a blender. Add oil in a slow stream, processing only until blended. Yields 3/4 cup.

Each serving contains:

Calories	270	Protein	20.3g
Carbohydrates	10g	Total fats	17.0g
		(Saturated fat 3.0g)	

Lion Inn Heritage Salad ▶

MIDDLE EASTERN TABBOULEH SALAD

HADDON HALL

You will want to add this delicious minty salad borrowed from Arabic cuisine to your collection. The chef often serves this dish with Belgian endive, or pita wedges that have been baked in a 200°F oven until crisp.

1 cup bulgar wheat
hot water to cover bulgar wheat
1/4 cup fresh mint, chopped (or 1 1/2 tablespoons dried mint)
1/2 cup fresh parsley, chopped
1/2 cup onion, finely diced
1/2 cup tomatoes, seeded and chopped
1/2 cup cucumber, seeded and diced
1/2 cup green onion, thinly sliced
4 tablespoons lemon juice
4 tablespoons olive oil
1 teaspoon chili powder
1 teaspoon ground coriander
1 teaspoon ground cumin

Place bulgar wheat in a bowl (if using dried mint, add to wheat now), add hot water to cover and soak for 1 hour. Combine fresh mint, parsley, onion, tomatoes, cucumber and green onion. Stir into bulgar. Whisk together lemon juice, olive oil, chili powder, coriander and cumin and stir into salad. For best flavour, allow to marinate 2 hours at room temperature or 24 to 48 hours in the refrigerator. Will keep up to 10 days refrigerated (stir daily). Serve cold. Serves 4 to 6.

Each serving contains:

Calories	*178*	*Protein*	*3.9g*
Carbohydrates	*21.9g*	*Total fats*	*9.6g*
		(Saturated fat 1.3g)	

GREEN SALAD WITH RASPBERRY VINAIGRETTE

COOPER'S INN & RESTAURANT

Owner and chef Allan Redmond has created an oil-free vinaigrette for this special salad. He finds that using 4 or 5 different greens gives a variety of taste, texture and colour, while using leaf lettuce gives the salad height and a nice appearance on the plate.

salad greens (variety of romaine, green and red leaf, radicchio, sprouts etc.), to serve 6
1/4 cup raspberry vinegar
1 tablespoon sugar
1 clove garlic, minced
1 teaspoon Worcestershire sauce
1 teaspoon Dijon mustard
1 teaspoon lemon juice
salt and pepper, to taste
1/2 cup water
Parmesan cheese
black pepper, freshly ground
1/4 cup raisins
lemon slices, fresh raspberries and capers, for garnish

Prepare salad greens and reserve. Combine vinegar, sugar, garlic, Worcestershire sauce, mustard, lemon juice, salt and pepper in a blender. Add water and process until vinaigrette is well blended.

Toss the greens with a little of the vinaigrette and place on individual plates that have been sprinkled with Parmesan cheese and freshly ground pepper. Sprinkle with raisins and garnish with a slice of lemon, a few fresh raspberries and capers. Serves 6.

Each serving contains:

Calories	*58*	*Protein*	*3.2g*
Carbohydrates	*10.0g*	*Total fats*	*1.3g*
		(Saturated fat 0.6g)	

Middle Eastern Tabbouleh Salad ▶

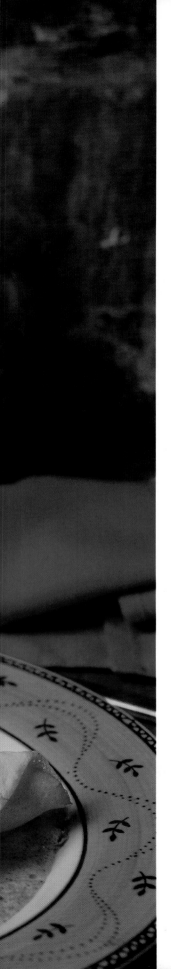

LIGHT FARE

There never seems to be enough time for a restful lunch. People traditionally treat this meal as a quick break to replenish their bodies with enough energy to last until dinner. Not surprisingly, those who take the time find the midday meal an ideal setting for relaxation and casual reunions with family and friends.

Our contacts in the restaurant industry are creating wonderful luncheon dishes for their patrons. They are eager to share a variety of these special vegetarian, ethnic and healthy recipes. We suggest you try Bellhill Tea House's Ratatouille en Croute or Acton's Petatou. Served with salad and crusty bread, they make an excellent main course.

◀ *Curried Vegetable Crêpes*

CURRIED VEGETABLE CRÊPES

SWEET BASIL BISTRO

At Sweet Basil Bistro, Chef Jakob Sandblom serves his crêpes with a rich creamy sauce. We tested the recipe by replacing the cream with milk and found that it did not compromise the dish. This is an ideal luncheon dish and we found it especially appealing when served with chutney, fresh coconut and slices of banana.

Crêpes:

1 egg + 1 egg white
1 cup milk
1 cup flour, sifted
pinch dried oregano
pinch turmeric
1 tablespoon vegetable oil

Prepare batter by whisking together all ingredients in a large bowl. Cover with plastic wrap and refrigerate 2 hours.

Brush a non-stick skillet or crêpe pan with a little vegetable oil and bring to medium-high heat. Add a scant 1/4 cup batter to barely cover the bottom of the pan and cook for approximately 30 seconds. Flip crêpe and cook another 15 seconds. Repeat, setting crêpes aside to cool. Yields 10 to 12 6-inch crêpes.

Filling:

4 ounces eggplant, peeled and cut into thin strips
4 ounces zucchini, cut into thin strips
1 large yellow onion, peeled and cut into thin strips
4 ounces sweet red and green pepper, seeds and ribs removed and cut into thin strips
2 tablespoons vegetable oil
2-3 tablespoons medium hot Madras curry paste
1/4 cup cream
salt and pepper, to taste

Sauce:

1 large clove garlic, chopped
2-3 whole star anise
1 tablespoon vegetable oil
1 1/2-2 tablespoons medium hot Madras curry paste
1 1/2 cups cream or milk
1/3 cup lemon juice
1 tablespoon chicken soup base mix (optional)
pinch dried cumin seeds
3/4 tablespoon cornstarch, dissolved in a little cold water

Prepare vegetables and set aside. In a large skillet, heat oil and sauté vegetables until barely tender, approximately 5 minutes. Stir in curry paste and cream, and cool until slightly thickened. Season with salt and pepper.

Briefly sauté garlic and star anise in oil over medium heat. Add curry paste, cumin seed, and soup base. Stir and heat for a few seconds. Stir in cream or milk and bring to a low boil. Add lemon juice and thicken with cornstarch mixture. Simmer 10 minutes, then remove from heat and strain.

Preheat oven to 350°F. Spoon a small amount of vegetable mixture into middle of each crêpe. Roll and place, seam side down, in a lightly greased baking dish. Spoon sauce over crêpes and place in oven to bring to serving temperature. Serves 4 to 6.

Each serving contains:

Calories	*291*	*Protein*	*8.6g*
Carbohydrates	*27.5g*	*Total fats*	*17.1g*
			(Saturated fat 5.4g)

ORANGE WHOLE WHEAT PANCAKES WITH BERRIES

ACACIA CROFT TEA ROOM AT PLANTERS' (BARRACKS) COUNTRY INN

Pancakes with a definite difference! The extra bonus with these pancakes is that they are healthy so you won't have to save them for a special occasion. We suggest using any fresh berry or combination of berries — whatever is in season!

1 1/2 cups whole wheat flour
1/4 teaspoon salt
2 teaspoons baking powder
1 1/4 cups orange juice
1 egg
1 cup small curd cottage cheese (lasagna style)
2 cups fresh berries, presweetened with sugar
   or honey
heavy cream, whipped (optional)

Sift together flour, salt and baking powder. Beat together orange juice and egg. Add liquid to dry ingredients, mixing only until combined. Heat a griddle to 380°F and grease lightly. Use scant 1/4 cup batter for each pancake. Bake pancakes until surface is covered with bubbles, turn and bake other side until golden. Yields 12 pancakes.

Stack 3 pancakes on each of 4 serving plates and fill each layer with 2 tablespoons cottage cheese and a covering of berries. Top with remaining berries and whipped cream. Serves 4.

Each serving contains:
Calories	288	*Protein*	16.5g
Carbohydrates	50.8g	*Total fats*	3.6g
		(Saturated fat 1.3g)	

POTATO & BUTTERNUT SQUASH CAKES

CHARLOTTE LANE CAFÉ & CRAFTS

This tasty little vegetarian delight can also be served as an appetizer or as a vegetable accompaniment to meat entrées.

1/2 pound butternut squash
1 large or 2 medium potatoes (dry/low starch
   variety)
1/4 ounce fresh coriander, chopped
2 ounces Cheddar cheese, grated
1/4 cup Parmesan cheese
1/4 teaspoon paprika
1/8 teaspoon nutmeg, ground
salt and pepper, to taste
flour, for dusting
olive oil

Preheat oven to 400°F. Peel and cut squash and potato into medium-sized pieces. Steam in a double boiler until soft. Dry for a few minutes in hot oven until steam on surface has dried. Mash potato and squash with a potato masher until smooth; stir in both cheeses, coriander and seasoning. Shape into small cakes and dust with flour. Heat a skillet, add a coating of olive oil and sauté cakes on both sides until golden brown.

Serve on a bed of spinach, garnished with a sprig of coriander. Accompany cakes with hot pepper jelly, mango chutney or salsa. Serves 4.

Each serving contains:
Calories	169	*Protein*	7.2g
Carbohydrates	13g	*Total fats*	9.8g
		(Saturated fat 4.4g)	

SPANAKOPITA

BELLHILL TEA HOUSE & GIFT SHOP

This delicious phyllo encrusted cheese and spinach dish is borrowed from traditional Greek cuisine. It's a specialty at Bellhill Tea House and embodies their philosophy of using only wholesome, natural ingredients.

1 package phyllo pastry, thawed
2 12-ounce packages fresh spinach
1 cup onion, chopped
3 tablespoons butter
2 cups feta cheese, crumbled
2 cups cottage cheese
5 eggs, beaten
1 teaspoon dried basil
1/2 teaspoon dried oregano
pepper, to taste
2 tablespoons flour
1/2 to 2/3 cup butter, melted (may use 1/2 butter and 1/2 olive oil)
fresh dill, dill seeds or fennel seeds, for topping

Preheat oven to 375°F. In a saucepan, cook spinach lightly, drain well and chop. In a skillet sauté onion in butter until soft. Mix spinach, onion, feta and cottage cheeses, eggs and seasonings in a large bowl and stir to combine. Lightly sprinkle flour over mixture and stir.

Line a 9-inch x 13-inch pan with foil. Place 1 phyllo sheet into the pan, making sure it extends over the edges; brush with melted butter. Repeat this process using 1/2 of the phyllo. Pour cheese mixture into pan and spread evenly to edges. Top with remaining phyllo, brushing each sheet with melted butter. Fold in edges neatly. Butter top layer and sprinkle with dill seeds, fennel seeds or sprigs of fresh dill.

Bake, uncovered, for 35 to 45 minutes until golden. Remove from oven, rest 5 to 10 minutes and cut into squares. Serves 6 to 8.

Each serving contains:

Calories	*356*	*Protein*	*18.8g*
Carbohydrates	*10.1g*	*Total fats*	*27.4g*
			(Saturated fat 13.1g)

Spanakopita ▶

46

EGG-WHITE OMELETTE WITH SPINACH & MUSHROOM

KELTIC LODGE

Keltic Lodge likes to provide appetizing meal selections for guests with special dietary requests. This healthy omelette made with egg whites is a wonderful recipe for those seeking cholesterol reduced fare.

3-4 egg whites
salt and pepper, to taste
small amount of butter, to coat skillet
3 tablespoons spinach, cooked and well
   drained
2-3 mushrooms, sliced

In a bowl, whisk egg whites until frothy; add salt and pepper to taste. Heat a large teflon skillet over high heat and add enough butter to lightly coat bottom of pan. Pour in egg mixture and shake pan until egg sets. Sprinkle spinach and mushrooms across centre of omelette. Remove from heat and, using a spatula, lift one third of omelette and fold over centre; repeat with other third of omelette. Tilt skillet and roll omelette onto a plate. Serves 1.

Each serving contains:

Calories	*116*	*Protein*	*15.5g*
Carbohydrates	*4.3g*	*Total fats*	*4.1g*
		(Saturated fat 2.4g)	

PENNE PASTA WITH SUN-DRIED TOMATO SAUCE

THE SHADOW LAWN COUNTRY INN

Sun-dried tomatoes, available in most large supermarkets and specialty food stores, are intensely flavoured and sweet. They add a rich flavour to a variety of dishes and are the key ingredient in this pasta sauce.

8 ounces penne pasta, cooked *al dente*
1/2 cup sun-dried tomatoes
1/2 cup white wine
6 large mushrooms, sliced
1 medium onion, chopped
1 stalk celery, chopped
1/4 cup green pepper, diced
1/4 cup red pepper, diced
2 teaspoons olive oil
1 teaspoon sugar
salt and pepper, to taste
2 teaspoons fresh oregano (1/2 teaspoon
   dried)
1/2 cup plain low-fat yoghurt
1/4 cup Parmesan cheese, for garnish

Prepare pasta, drain and keep warm. While pasta is cooking, marinate sun-dried tomatoes in wine to reconstitute, then chop. Sauté mushrooms, onion, celery and peppers in olive oil over medium heat until crisp-tender. Add tomatoes, wine, sugar and seasonings. Turn off heat, add yoghurt and toss with penne pasta. Top with a sprinkling of Parmesan cheese for garnish. Serves 4.

Each serving contains:

Calories	*331*	*Protein*	*13.1g*
Carbohydrates	*54.1g*	*Total fats*	*5.2g*
		(Saturated fat 1.5g)	

ZUCCHINI SUPREME

THE WHITMAN INN

It has become a challenge for chefs to find recipes for the popular and prolific zucchini. This tasty vegetarian treat from the kitchen of Nancy Gurnham can be served as a luncheon dish or cut in smaller portions and used as a vegetable accompaniment to a main course entrée.

3-4 medium zucchini, thinly sliced
    (approximately 5 cups)
1/2 cup green pepper, diced
1/2 cup onion, diced
3 eggs, beaten
3/4 cup mayonnaise, homemade or other
    good quality
3/4 cup Parmesan cheese, freshly grated
1/2 teaspoon celery seed
1 teaspoon oregano
1/2 teaspoon thyme
soft buttered breadcrumbs and additional
    Parmesan cheese, grated, for topping

Preheat oven to 350°F. Steam zucchini slices for 2 to 3 minutes to soften. Combine zucchini, green pepper and onion in a large bowl. Blend together beaten eggs, mayonnaise, Parmesan cheese and seasoning, and stir into vegetables. Pour mixture into shallow, greased 2-quart baking dish. Top with breadcrumbs and additional Parmesan cheese and bake in oven 30 to 40 minutes until set and browned on top. Remove from oven and rest 10 minutes before serving. Serves 6.

Each serving contains:

Calories	308	Protein	8.8g
Carbohydrates	6.4g	Total fats	28.3g
		(Saturated fat 6.4g)	

RATATOUILLE WITH TUNA

THE WALKER INN

Theresa Walker of the Walker Inn serves this delightful combination of fresh vegetables and tuna in a puffed pastry shell or over steamed rice.

1-2 tablespoons olive oil
1 large onion, chopped
2 medium zucchinis, quartered and sliced
2 large tomatoes, cubed
1/2 green pepper, diced
1/3 cup red wine
1/3 cup vegetable broth
1/2 teaspoon garlic salt
dash pepper
1/2 teaspoon thyme
1/2 teaspoon basil
2 cans water-packed tuna, drained

Heat olive oil over medium heat and sauté onion, zucchini, tomatoes and green pepper for 5 minutes. Add wine, broth, garlic salt, pepper, thyme and basil, reduce heat, cover and cook until vegetables are softened and mixture has thickened. Add drained tuna, return to serving temperature and serve in baked puff-pastry shells or over steamed rice. Serves 4 to 6.

Each serving contains:

Calories	179	Protein	22.1g
Carbohydrates	9.4g	Total fats	4.7g
		(Saturated fat 0.8g)	

RATATOUILLE EN CROUTE

BELLHILL TEA HOUSE & GIFT SHOP

This wholesome and nutritious vegetarian entrée works well as a luncheon dish. It can also be served with a salad to make a delicious meatless evening meal.

Whole Wheat Crust:

1 package yeast
1/4 cup warm water
1 tablespoon honey
1/2 teaspoon salt
1 1/2 cups all-purpose, white flour
2 eggs
1/4 cup whole wheat flour
1/2 cup butter, softened
eggwash (1 egg beaten with 1 teaspoon water),
    for assembling croute

Ratatouille:

1/4 cup olive oil
1 eggplant, unpeeled and cut in 1/2-inch
    cubes (approximately 1 pound)
1 medium onion, slivered
1/2 pound mushrooms, thinly sliced
1 green or red pepper, julienned
1 clove garlic, minced
1 pound tinned tomatoes, drained and
    chopped (or equivalent fresh, chopped)
3/4 teaspoon dried basil
3/4 teaspoon dried oregano
1/8 teaspoon black pepper
pinch of cayenne pepper
2 eggs, beaten
1/4 cup Parmesan cheese, grated
1 cup Swiss cheese, grated

To make crust, add warm water to a large bowl, sprinkle yeast over top and let stand until bubbly. Stir in honey and salt and 1/2 cup of the white flour. Beat at medium speed approximately 3 minutes. Beat in eggs one at a time, then gradually beat in whole wheat flour and remaining white flour. Add butter, 2 tablespoons at a time, beating well after each addition. Remove dough to a greased bowl, cover and let rise in a warm place. When doubled in bulk, approximately 1 hour, punch down.

Prepare ratatouille while dough is rising. Heat olive oil over medium heat and cook eggplant and onion until vegetables are soft, approximately 10 minutes. Add mushrooms, peppers, garlic, tomatoes and spices. Bring to a boil, reduce heat and simmer, stirring occasionally until mixture is reduced to 4 cups. Remove from heat and let stand 10 minutes. Mix together beaten eggs and cheeses and stir into vegetable mixture.

To assemble croute: roll out 2/3 of dough on a floured surface. Line a greased 8-inch springform pan with dough and brush with eggwash. Fill pan with ratatouille and fold edges inward. Roll remaining dough in a 9-inch circle and place over filling. Moisten edges with eggwash, seal and let rise 30 minutes. Preheat oven to 375°F. Brush top with remaining eggwash and bake 1 hour. If the top becomes too brown, cover loosely with foil. Remove from oven and let stand 15 minutes before removing sides. Serve warm or at room temperature. Serves 8 to 10.

Each serving contains:

Calories	*268*	*Protein*	*8.7g*
Carbohydrates	*20.5g*	*Total fats*	*17.3g*
		(Saturated fat 7.9g)	

ACTON'S PETATOU

ACTON'S GRILL & CAFÉ

The chef at Acton's suggests you use extra virgin olive oil in this dish. Extra virgin oil is the result of the first pressing of the olives and is the finest and fruitiest of the olive oils.

1 pound small new potatoes, washed and
  unpeeled
1 sprig fresh dill
2 bay leaves
1/3 cup extra virgin olive oil
3 tablespoons white wine vinegar
2 tablespoons shallots, chopped fine
2 tablespoons fresh basil, chopped
1 tablespoon fresh thyme, chopped
salt and pepper, to taste
4 egg yolks
4 ounces cream goat cheese (chèvre)
assorted greens, to serve 4

Cook potatoes, dill and bay leaves in boiling water until barely tender. Drain and cool to a handling temperature. Peel potatoes, slice in 1/4-inch slices and reserve.

Prepare dressing by whisking together the oil, vinegar, shallots, basil, thyme, and salt and pepper. Set aside 1/4 cup of dressing in a separate container.

Preheat oven to 400°F. Whisk 2 egg yolks into the remaining dressing then gently toss with potatoes to evenly coat. Layer potato slices, overlapping slightly, in a greased 9-inch pie plate. Bake 20 minutes, or until potatoes are tender. Beat together goat cheese and remaining egg yolks. Spread over top of the potatoes and broil until golden, approximately 2 to 3 minutes.

To serve, toss greens with reserved 1/4 cup dressing and divide amongst 4 serving plates. Cut potato petatou into wedges and serve on the greens. Serves 4.

Each serving contains:

Calories	*390*	*Protein*	*14.9g*
Carbohydrates	*24.7g*	*Total fats*	*27.4g*
		(Saturated fat 8.8g)	

SEAFOOD

Our close proximity to the seafood-rich waters of the cold North Atlantic gives our chefs an opportunity to experiment with the varied ocean species available to them.

In this book you will find recipes for salmon, white fish and, of course, our famed Digby scallops. We are particularly pleased with recipes like the Sunshine Café's Pesce Alla Pizzaiola and The Walker Inn's Fresh Atlantic Tuna, which feature seafood less frequently tried in Maritime kitchens.

◀ *Campfire Rainbow Trout with Spinach Sauce*

CAMPFIRE RAINBOW TROUT WITH SPINACH SAUCE

THE INN AT BAY FORTUNE

Chef Michael Smith excels in cooking artistry when he prepares this recipe for trout and Spinach Sauce accompanied by a Smoked Salmon Bread Pudding.

6 rainbow trout
salt and pepper, to taste
2 cups cornmeal
3 tablespoons butter

Filet trout and remove bones, leaving skin intact. Season with salt and pepper and dredge skin sides in cornmeal. Pan fry in butter in a heavy skillet until skin is crisp and fish is almost done, approximately 8 minutes. Carefully turn fish over and cook until fish flakes easily and is opaque. Serve immediately, drizzled with Spinach Sauce. Serves 6.

Spinach Sauce:

1 small onion, finely diced
1/3 cup extra virgin olive oil
2-3 cloves garlic, minced
1/2 teaspoon nutmeg
1 pound fresh spinach, stems removed and
    rinsed
1/2 cup white wine
salt and pepper, to taste

Sweat onions in olive oil over medium heat until soft. Add garlic and sprinkle with nutmeg. Add prepared spinach and wine; stir vigorously until spinach wilts completely and turns bright green. Purée spinach mixture in a blender and strain through a fine mesh sieve. Season with salt and pepper, reheat and serve immediately. Yields 1 cup.

Each serving contains:

Calories	*340*	*Protein*	*22.2g*
Carbohydrates	*24.7g*	*Total fats*	*15.7g*
		(Saturated fat 2.3g)	

Smoked Salmon Bread Pudding:

6 slices rye bread, toasted and cubed
1 cup blend (12% m.f.)
3 eggs
8 ounces smoked salmon, julienned
2 ounces fresh dill, minced
1 lemon, zest and juice reserved
1 tablespoon Dijon mustard
salt and pepper, to taste.

Preheat oven to 350°F. Toast bread slices until golden brown and cut into cubes. In a large bowl whisk together the blend, eggs, dill, lemon juice, zest, Dijon, salt and pepper. Slice salmon and add with the bread cubes to custard base. Let stand 20 minutes, allowing the bread to absorb the base completely. Butter, then flour, 6 individual baking dishes or 1 large baking dish. Divide mixture amongst baking dishes and bake until firm, approximately 25 minutes. Serve with Rainbow Trout and Spinach Sauce. Serves 6.

Each serving contains:

Calories	*220*	*Protein*	*14.2g*
Carbohydrates	*19.4g*	*Total fats*	*9.9g*
		(Saturated fat 4.2g)	

LOIN OF COD WITH MUSHROOM SPINACH SAUCE

AUBERGE LE VIEUX PRESBYTERE DE BOUCTOUCHE 1880 LTÉE

Marcelle Albert serves this elegant cod entrée with steamed parsleyed potatoes and seasonal vegetables.

2 pounds cod fillets
cornstarch or flour, for dredging
salt and pepper
butter and oil, for sautéeing

Mushroom Spinach Sauce:

4 tablespoons butter
1/3 cup onion, finely diced
8 ounces mushrooms, chopped
1 1/4 cups chicken stock
8 ounces cooked spinach, well-drained and
    chopped
2 tablespoons cornstarch, diluted in cold
    water
2/3 cup heavy cream (35% m.f.)
salt and pepper, to taste

Melt butter in heavy-bottomed skillet and fry onion until soft. Add the mushrooms and cook until the juices start to run. Add chicken stock and spinach and mix well. Blend cornstarch with small amount of cold water and stir into mushroom mixture. Simmer gently to thicken. Stir in the cream and keep warm.

Remove any bones from the cod and cut in serving-size pieces. Combine flour, salt and pepper. Dredge fish in flour. Heat butter and oil in a skillet and quickly sauté cod, turning once. Fish is cooked when it flakes easily and is opaque. Arrange fish on serving plates and top with Mushroom Spinach Sauce. Serves 6.

Each serving contains:

Calories	352	Protein	30.9g
Carbohydrates	8.9g	Total fats	21.6g
		(Saturated fat 11.6g)	

THE DOCTOR'S INN SALMON WITH GREEN PEPPERCORNS

THE DOCTOR'S INN

Paul Offer of the Doctor's Inn coaxes the large black woodstove he affectionately calls "Leaping Hannah" into service each evening as he prepares dinner for his guests. The Salmon with Green Peppercorns is a house speciality and is accompanied by fresh produce from Offer's extensive gardens.

4 6-ounce salmon steaks
4 teaspoons green peppercorns
1/2 tablespoon vegetable oil
1 lime, sliced, for garnish
fresh dill, for garnish

Choose compact salmon steaks, cut about 1 inch thick. Spoon 1/2 teaspoon of peppercorns and their liquid over each steak and press peppercorns into the flesh. Heat oil over medium-high heat in a large skillet. Brown steaks. While steaks are cooking, cover the top of each steak with remaining peppercorns and liquid. Turn and cook until fish flakes easily and flesh is opaque. Serve garnished with fresh lime slices and fresh dill. Serves 4.

Each serving contains:

Calories	219	Protein	34.9g
Carbohydrates	8.8g	Total fats	7.6g
		(Saturated fat 1.0g)	

WHITE POINT BEACH LODGE SALMON IN PARCHMENT

WHITE POINT BEACH LODGE

Chef Chris Profit prepares these little packets of salmon and colourful vegetables in individual portions. We found that they make an excellent entrée to prepare in advance. Simply pop them in the oven 20 minutes before serving time.

4 sheets parchment paper, approximately
    8 inches by 8 inches
4 salmon fillets, boneless and skinless (6
    ounces each)
2 cups mixed vegetables (carrots, leeks, celery,
    red or green peppers etc.), in matchstick
    strips
1 teaspoon lemon pepper
1 teaspoon tarragon
dash of salt
1 lemon, cut in 8 wedges

Preheat oven to 375°F. Place a salmon fillet in the centre of each square of parchment paper. Choose a colourful assortment of vegetables and divide between salmon packets. Sprinkle with lemon pepper, tarragon and salt, and top with lemon wedges. Fold paper over salmon, pinching fold to create a seal. Your packet should be larger than its contents to allow space for a build-up of steam. Bake at 375°F for 15 to 20 minutes, depending upon the thickness of the salmon. Serves 4.

Each serving contains:
Calories	227	Protein	34.9g
Carbohydrates	8.8g	Total fats	6.1g
		(Saturated fat 1.0g)	

SALMON FILLETS WITH FRESH ROSEMARY

SEASONS IN THYME

Fresh rosemary is an herb sent from heaven! In this dish it heightens but doesn't overpower the delicate flavour of the fresh Atlantic salmon.

4 5-ounce salmon fillets, boneless and skinless
2 teaspoons fresh rosemary, chopped
1 pound fresh green beans, french-cut
salt and pepper, to season
1 tablespoon safflower or olive oil
1 large tomato, peeled and chopped
fresh herbs (rosemary, purple basil etc.), for
    garnish

Rinse and pat dry the salmon fillets. Rub with rosemary leaves and refrigerate, covered, 2 hours. At serving time, trim green beans and cook in a little salted water only until crisp-tender. Drain and keep warm.

In a large skillet, heat oil over medium-high heat. Season fillets with salt and pepper. Sear in pan, turning once. Remove salmon from pan and bake in the oven for 7 minutes. Wipe oil from skillet with paper towelling and simmer chopped tomato for 2 to 3 minutes. Serve salmon fillets with bundles of green beans, topped with a spoonful of tomato and garnished with fresh herbs. Serves 4.

Each serving contains:
Calories	237	Protein	30.6g
Carbohydrates	9.9g	Total fats	8.6g
		(Saturated fat 1.3g)	

Salmon Fillets with Fresh Rosemary ▶

PESCE ALLA PIZZAIOLA (WHITE FISH WITH TOMATO & GARLIC SAUCE)

SUNSHINE CAFÉ

We like to prepare this dish when the tomatoes are plentiful in the garden and the fresh herbs are at their peak.

6 portions fresh, boneless fish (monkfish, shark, halibut etc.)
2-3 tablespoons extra virgin olive oil
3 tablespoons dry white wine
Marinade (recipe follows)
Tomato Sauce (recipe follows)

Pour marinade into a shallow glass dish, add fish portions and turn several times to coat well. Cover and refrigerate 1 to 2 hours.

Preheat oven to 350°F. Pour olive oil in a large heavy skillet and heat to high. Remove fish from marinade, dry off and place in skillet. Cook on each side for 2 minutes. Remove fish from skillet, place in a warmed ovenproof casserole and bake until fish flakes and is opaque, approximately 6 to 8 minutes. Meanwhile, deglaze skillet with white wine and 3 tablespoons of marinade. Add tomato sauce and reheat. To serve, pour sauce over fish portions. Serves 6.

Marinade:

4 tablespoons extra virgin olive oil
zest from 1 lemon
juice from 1/2 lemon
1 tablespoon fresh Italian parsley, finely chopped (1 teaspoon dried)
1 tablespoon fresh basil, finely chopped (1 teaspoon dried)
pepper, freshly ground (3 good twists of peppermill)

Whisk all ingredients in a bowl until emulsified. Yields 1/2 cup.

Tomato Sauce:

2 tablespoons extra virgin olive oil
4 cloves garlic, minced
2 shallots, finely diced
4 anchovy fillets, finely chopped
1/4 cup dry white wine
4 cups chopped fresh tomatoes, skinned and seeded
1 teaspoon fresh oregano, chopped (or 1/2 teaspoon dried)
salt and pepper, to taste

Heat olive oil in a heavy-bottomed saucepan, add garlic, shallots and anchovies, and sauté gently until translucent. Deglaze pan with wine and add tomatoes and oregano. Season with salt and pepper and simmer until tomatoes are cooked, approximately 5 to 8 minutes. Remove from heat and purée in a food processor. Reserve. Yields 3 cups.

Each serving contains:

Calories	238	*Protein*	23.4g
Carbohydrates	7.9g	*Total fats*	11.5g
			(Saturated fat 1.6g)

PASTA WITH SEAFOOD & PESTO

THE GALLEY

The chef tells us that you may use any choice of pasta in this dish, and the amount of pesto you use will depend upon individual taste. To store leftover pesto, place in a sterilized jar and cover with a thin film of olive oil. Cover tightly and refrigerate for up to two months, or freeze for up to a year.

10 ounces fettucini, *or* pasta of choice, cooked
 al dente
1 pound fresh seafood (scallops, shrimp,
 monkfish, halibut, haddock or lobster), in
 bite-sized pieces
1 tablespoon vegetable oil
Pesto Sauce (recipe follows)
lemon wedges, fresh basil leaves and chopped
 sun-dried tomatoes, for garnish (optional)

Heat oil in a large skillet. Add seafood pieces and partially cook, about 1 to 2 minutes. Remove from heat and add 1/2 to 3/4 cup Pesto Sauce and well-drained pasta, tossing to combine. Return to burner to ensure that seafood is cooked and pasta is hot. Garnish plates with lemon wedges, fresh basil leaves or slivers of sun-dried tomatoes. Serves 4.

Pesto Sauce:

We suggest making Pesto Sauce when fresh basil is plentiful. This is a multi-use sauce, ideal for salad dressings and soups, or, when combined with a little mayonnaise, for a vegetable dip.

1/4 cup pine nuts (optional)
2 cups fresh basil, washed and stems removed
 (about 3 bunches)
4 large sprigs parsley, stems removed
2-3 cloves garlic, minced
1/4 cup Parmesan cheese
1/2 teaspoon pepper, freshly ground
1/2 cup olive oil

Place pine nuts, basil, parsley, garlic, cheese and pepper in a food processor fitted with a metal blade. Process until mixture is finely chopped and smooth. With processor still running, add oil in a thin stream. Process a further few seconds. Yields 1 cup.

Each serving contains:

Calories	*552*	*Protein*	*36.4g*
Carbohydrates	*56.8g*	*Total fats*	*21.6g*
		(Saturated fat 3.1g)	

CURRIED ROSE FISH POACHED IN COCONUT MILK

HADDON HALL

The chef at Haddon Hall marries the subtle flavour of coconut with the exotic flavours of curry and cardamon to prepare this beautiful rosy fillet of perch. We suggest serving this dish with steamed basmati rice and fresh spring vegetables.

1 coconut
1/2 small onion, diced
1 large clove garlic, diced
1 tablespoon extra virgin olive oil
1/2 teaspoon lemon juice
1 teaspoon curry
pinch chili powder
pinch cardamon
4 5-ounce ocean perch fillets
2 apples, halved and cored, for garnish

Remove milk and meat from coconut and set aside. Sweat onion and garlic in olive oil until tender. Deglaze pan with lemon juice, being careful to scrape up any small bits in the bottom of the pan. Add coconut milk and simmer.

Combine curry, chili and cardamon in a small bowl. Sprinkle fillets with spices and place in simmering liquid for 2 to 3 minutes until fish is opaque and flakes easily. Remove from heat. Divide perch and sauce amongst 4 serving plates. Garnish with a fan of fresh apples. Serves 4.

Each serving contains:

Calories	*253*	*Protein*	*27.3g*
Carbohydrates	*2.5g*	*Total fats*	*12.9g*
			(Saturated fat 1.2g)

HADDOCK FILLETS WITH PEACH & PEPPER SALSA

BLUENOSE LODGE

Grace Swan of the Bluenose Lodge tells us that this colourful salsa turns a fish fillet into a gourmet feast. We couldn't agree more.

1 1/2-pound fillet of haddock (or white fish of choice)
1 egg, beaten
1/2 cup dry breadcrumbs
2 teaspoons butter
salt and pepper, to taste

Cut haddock into 4 serving pieces, being careful to remove any bones. Dip in egg, coat with breadcrumbs and season with salt and pepper. Melt butter in a skillet and cook fillets, turning once, until fish flakes and is opaque. Serve garnished with Peach & Pepper Salsa. Serves 4.

Peach & Pepper Salsa:

1/2 cup fresh peaches, finely diced
1/4 cup onion, finely diced
1/2 cup red pepper, finely diced
1 teaspoon jalapeno pepper, finely diced (or 2 shakes Tabasco sauce)
1 tablespoon fresh cilantro or parsley, chopped
1 tablespoon lime juice

Combine all ingredients and refrigerate 1 to 2 hours to blend flavours. Yields 1 1/4 cups.

Each serving contains:

Calories	*200*	*Protein*	*34.3g*
Carbohydrates	*4.4g*	*Total fats*	*4.4g*
			(Saturated fat 1.8g)

Curried Rose Fish Poached in Coconut Milk ▶

THAI FISH ROLLS

SWEET BASIL BISTRO

Rice paper and fish sauce (or nam pla *as it is often called), are available in most Asian speciality stores. The chef tells us that the spinach, lettuce and basil leaves provide mositure in the rolls.*

12 sheets 8-inch rice paper
6 ounces shrimps, cooked and shelled
6 ounces scallops
6 ounces haddock or other white fish
2 tablespoons fresh lime juice
2 tablespoons fish sauce *(nam pla)*
dash red pepper sauce
salt and pepper, to taste
6 large leaves spinach, rinsed
6 medium leaves Bibb lettuce
6 large leaves fresh basil

Dipping Sauce:

1/2 cup fish sauce *(nam pla)*
1/4 cup oyster sauce
1/4 cup fresh lime juice
1/2 tablespoon cornstarch, dissolved in 1/4
   cup cold water

Lay rice paper in cold water to soften enough to be pliable. Tear seafood into small pieces and combine in a large mixing bowl. Gently stir in lime juice, fish sauce and hot pepper sauce. Season with salt and pepper.

Arrange each sheet of rice paper on a flat surface. Lay a leaf of spinach, lettuce and basil on each sheet. Spread fish mixture down the center of each sheet and roll, tucking in ends to form a cylinder. Steam rolls on a rack over boiling water, approximately 6 minutes. While rolls are steaming, combine dipping sauce ingredients in a small saucepan and bring to a low boil. Reduce heat and simmer 1 minute. To serve, place warm rolls in dipping sauce. Serves 6.

Each serving contains:
Calories	*150*	*Protein*	*18.2g*
Carbohydrates	*11g*	*Total fats*	*4.2g*
			(Saturated fat 1.2g)

Thai Fish Rolls ▶

SEAFOOD PAELLA

THE PANSY PATCH

Paella, which takes its name from the two handled pan in which it is prepared and traditionally served, is a marvellous blend of stock, vegetables, seafood and rice. We are sure The Pansy Patch rendition will become a family favourite.

1 teaspoon vegetable oil
1 cup long grain rice
1 teaspoon curry
1 teaspoon salt
2 cups chicken stock or water
1 clove garlic, minced
1 small red onion, thinly sliced
1/2 red pepper, in julienne strips
1/2 green pepper, in julienne strips
1 cup broccoli florets
1/2 pound snow peas, ends cut and strings
    removed
12 large shrimp, raw
9-12 large scallops
9-12 fresh mussels, scrubbed and debearded
1 pound haddock fillets, in bite-sized chunks
2-3 tablespoons oyster sauce
2-3 tablespoons white wine

Place oil in a saucepan and brown rice over medium heat for 2 to 3 minutes. Stir in curry, and continue to cook 1 minute, stirring constantly. Add salt and water, cover and bring to a boil. Immediately reduce heat and simmer 20 minutes or until rice is tender and all the liquid is absorbed.

Spray a large skillet with a non-stick vegetable oil and sauté garlic and onion until slightly tender. Add shrimp and scallops and stir fry 1 minute. Stir in the remaining ingredients, cover and simmer until mussels have opened, about 5 to 6 minutes. To serve, spoon rice in the centre of serving plates and top with seafood and vegetables, discarding any mussels that have not opened. Serves 4 to 6.

Each serving contains:

Calories	*279*	*Protein*	*29.0g*
Carbohydrates	*32.2g*	*Total fats*	*2.8g*
		(Saturated fat 0.5g)	

Seafood Paella ▶

TUNA STEAKS WITH TOMATO TOPPING

THE WALKER INN

Theresa Walker accents her tuna steaks with a sauce of fresh tomatoes, olives and capers. She serves this filling dish accompanied by rice or potatoes.

4 6-ounce tuna steaks
1 teaspoon lemon juice
dash salt and pepper
1 tablespoon olive oil

Tomato Topping:

1 medium onion, sliced in rings
2 cloves garlic, crushed
1 tablespoon olive oil
6-8 medium tomatoes, cubed
salt and pepper, to taste
1 tablespoon fresh basil, chopped
   (1 teaspoon dried)
1 tablespoon fresh oregano, chopped (1
   teaspoon dried)
1/4 cup dry red wine
1 tablespoon capers
1 tablespoon green olives, sliced

Season steaks with lemon juice, salt and pepper. Pan-fry in olive oil, turning once, until fish is opaque and flakes easily.

Sauté onion rings and garlic in olive oil until onion is softened, about 5 minutes. Add tomato cubes and season with salt, pepper, basil and oregano. Simmer 5 minutes. Reduce heat, add red wine and cook for an additional 5 minutes to allow sauce to thicken slightly. Add capers and bring back to serving temperature. To serve, spoon sauce over tuna steaks and garnish with olive slices. Serves 4.

Each serving contains:
Calories	*334*	*Protein*	*41.6g*
Carbohydrates	*10.5g*	*Total fats*	*12.6g*
		(Saturated fat 2.7g)	

INN ON THE LAKE'S SEAFOOD CIOPPINO

INN ON THE LAKE

Food historians tell us that cioppino originated with the Italian immigrants in San Francisco. We suggest you serve this delicious fish stew with crusty bread and a tossed salad.

3 tablespoons butter
1/4 each green, red and yellow pepper,
   julienned
1 leek, white part only, cleaned and julienned
2 medium tomatoes, peeled, seeded and diced
1 1/2 cups white wine
1 1/2 cups chicken stock
8 large scallops
8 large shrimps
8 ounces haddock fillets, in chunks
8 ounces salmon fillets, in chunks
16 fresh mussels, scrubbed and debearded
salt and pepper, to taste
4 sprigs fresh parsley, chopped

Heat butter in a large skillet over medium heat. Add peppers and leeks and saute 2 minutes. Add tomatoes, wine and stock and bring to a boil. Add scallops, shrimps, haddock, salmon and fresh mussels. Simmer, covered, until fish is cooked and mussel shells are open. Season with salt and pepper and divide broth and seafood amongst 4 serving bowls; sprinkle with parsley. Serves 4.

Each serving contains:
Calories	*243*	*Protein*	*24.6g*
Carbohydrates	*7.2g*	*Total fats*	*8.4g*
		(Saturated fat 4.0g)	

LOBSTER & SCALLOPS WITH SUN-DRIED TOMATOES IN BASIL CREAM

DUNCREIGAN COUNTRY INN

This is a lighter version of a dish that appeared in our Lobster and Other Shellfish cookbook. Eleanor Mullendore of Duncreigan recognizes the trend towards healthier and lighter cooking and has revised the recipe for us. She serves it over sweet red pepper and spinach fettucini.

1/2 cup sun-dried tomatoes, refreshed in
  boiling water
3/4 pound large scallops
2 cooked lobster tails, split and shelled
3-4 minced shallots
1/2 cup dry white wine
4 tablespoons fresh basil leaves, chopped
4 ounces reduced-fat Swiss cheese, grated
1 cup White Sauce (recipe follows)
dash cayenne
salt and pepper, to taste
4 whole lobster claws, shelled, as garnish
additional fresh basil leaves, as garnish
fresh pasta to serve 4, cooked *al dente*

Reconstitute sun-dried tomatoes, drain and slice into thin strips. Poach scallops with minced shallots in the wine for 2 to 3 minutes. Add lobster tails and heat briefly. Remove shellfish and keep warm. Reduce wine slightly, then add chopped basil and sun-dried tomatoes. Stir in white sauce and heat on low, stirring constantly. Stir in grated cheese and continue to stir until cheese is melted. Add cayenne, salt and pepper. Arrange seafood over cooked pasta, top with sauce and garnish with a lobster claw and additional fresh basil leaves. Serves 4.

White Sauce: (supplied by authors)

1 tablespoon butter
1 scant tablespoon flour
1 cup 2% milk
dash salt and white pepper

Melt butter in a saucepan over medium heat. Whisk in flour and cook roux for 2 minutes, stirring constantly. Add milk and continue to stir until mixture thickens and bubbles. Season with salt and pepper. Yields 1 cup.

Each serving contains:

Calories	*278*	*Protein*	*34.1g*
Carbohydrates	*14.9g*	*Total fats*	*6.8g*
			(Saturated fat 3.6g)

MEATS

Diners in the Maritimes are becoming more adventurous, willing to stray from the traditional entrée into more exotic, international fare. Our Maritime chefs are nothing if not innovative and they delight in meeting their patrons' expectations. In sampling the fare offered by our inns and restaurants, we have found a variety of entrées suitable for family dining and for gala entertaining.

We particularly recommend the easily prepared Coconut Curry Penne from Charlotte Lane Café & Crafts, the elegant Stuffed Pork Tenderloin from Lunenburg's Lion Inn and Halliburton House's Chicken Camembert. The latter is a delicious pecan-and-cheese stuffed breast served with a creamy white wine sauce.

◄ *Chicken Camembert*

CHICKEN CAMEMBERT

HALLIBURTON HOUSE INN

This is an elegant entrée well-suited for a special occasion. The sauce is very rich and we suggest serving it from a sauce boat, thus allowing guests to decide upon their own level of decadence.

4 6-ounce boneless and skinless chicken breasts
4 tablespoons chopped pecans
4 tablespoons peeled and chopped apple
4 wedges Camembert cheese (1-inch size)
1/2 cup flour
2 eggs
2 tablespoons milk
3 cups fresh bread crumbs, seasoned
2 tablespoons vegetable oil
3/4 cup white wine
5 black peppercorns
1 sprig each thyme and parsley
1 bay leaf
1 1/2 cups heavy cream (32% m.f.)
1/4 red bell pepper, finely chopped
4 sprigs fresh parsley, for garnish

Preheat oven to 350ºF. Slice chicken breasts on thick side halfway through, to form a pocket. Place 1 tablespoon each of pecans and apple in breast pocket. Add wedge of cheese and press edges together to seal firmly. Dredge chicken in flour. Whip together egg and milk, coat breasts with egg mixture and then roll in bread crumbs. Brown chicken in hot oil, turning once. Finish in oven, 15 to 20 minutes.

In a medium saucepan, reduce wine, pepper-corns, thyme, parsley and bay leaf until mixture forms a thick glaze. Add cream and simmer over medium-low heat until desired consistency is reached, approximately 10 additional minutes. Remove herbs and bay leaf. To serve, nap breasts with sauce and garnish with finely chopped red pepper and parsley. Serves 4.

Each serving contains:

Calories	*643*	*Protein*	*41.4g*
Carbohydrates	*14.7g*	*Total fats*	*43.4g*
		(Saturated fat 21.5g)	

BAKED BREASTS OF CHICKEN

SUNSHINE CAFÉ

"Cooking, like all human activity can be raised to the level of art," says Chef Mark Gabrieau. With this dish he lives up to his motto and creates a delicious fruit chutney and an innovative chicken entrée.

6 chicken breasts, boneless and skinless
1 tablespoon olive oil
apricot halves *or* Mandarin orange segments
Sunshine Café Fresh Fruit Chutney (see page 122)

Preheat oven to 350ºF. Lightly brush olive oil in a hot skillet, then add chicken and sear on both sides. Do not cook through. Remove chicken from skillet and pat dry with paper towel. Place chicken on a baking sheet, spread chutney evenly over breasts and top with apricots or Mandarin oranges. Bake for 10 to 12 minutes or until cooked and no longer pink on the inside. Serves 6.

Each serving contains:

Calories	*173*	*Protein*	*21.3g*
Carbohydrates	*13.2g*	*Total fats*	*3.8g*
		(Saturated fat 0.7g)	

ROASTED CHICKEN BREASTS WITH CRANBERRY PORT SAUCE

THE PINES RESORT HOTEL

For this dish, the chef at The Pines likes to use boneless chicken breasts with the skin left on. He simply slides the stuffing between the skin and the breast. A healthier version would use boneless and skinless breasts, with the stuffing added to a pocket cut in the breast.

6 6-ounce boneless chicken breasts
1 1/2 tablespoons butter
1 small onion, finely chopped
12 ounces fresh mushrooms, finely chopped
2 small zucchini, grated and drained
1 teaspoon dried tarragon
1/4 cup heavy cream (32% m.f.)
1 1/2 tablespoons lemon juice
3 tablespoons breadcrumbs
2 tablespoons parsley, chopped
salt and pepper, to taste
2 tablespoons butter, softened

Sauce:

1/4 cup port wine
1/2 cup dry red wine
1/4 cup dried cranberries or currants
1 cup chicken stock
1 tablespoon butter

Preheat oven to 375°F. Trim chicken breasts of any fat. Heat butter in skillet over medium-high heat, then add onions and sauté until softened. Add mushrooms and zucchini and sauté, stirring occassionally, until all liquid has evaporated (approximately 10 minutes). Stir in tarragon and cream and continue to cook until cream has reduced and mixture is thick, approximately 5 minutes. Stir in lemon juice and add breadcrumbs to hold mixture together. Add parsley and season with salt and pepper.

With fingertips, make a pocket between skin and flesh of each breast, or, if using skinless breasts, make a pocket, being careful not to cut through. Divide stuffing and fill pockets.

Lightly grease a baking dish, preferably metal. Dot breasts with butter and bake until juices run clear, approximately 25 to 30 minutes. If cooking with the skin on, place under a broiler to crisp.

While chicken is baking, combine port, red wine, cranberries and chicken stock in a pot and bring to boil over medium-high heat. Reduce by half, skimming occasionally. Reduce heat to low and whisk in butter, 1 teaspoon at a time, until sauce is slightly thickened and glossy.

To serve, slice breasts diagonally on serving plate, napped with sauce and garnished with additional dried cranberries, if desired. Serves 6.

Each serving contains:

Calories	*332*	*Protein*	*25.1g*
Carbohydrates	*18.8g*	*Total fats*	*15.3g*
			(Saturated fat 8.5g)

CHICKEN BREAST FLAMBÉ

LITTLE SHEMOGUE COUNTRY INN

Owner and chef Petra Sudbrack often serves her flambéed chicken with a colourful fruit salad and basmati rice. We suggest you warm the brandy slightly before igniting.

4 tablespoons sunflower oil
2 tablespoons fresh rosemary, chopped
2 tablespoons fresh tarragon, chopped
salt and pepper, to taste
2 tablespoons butter
4 6-ounce boneless and skinless chicken
  breasts
1 ounce brandy
Fresh Fruit Salad, recipe follows

In a shallow dish, combine sunflower oil, rosemary, tarragon, salt and pepper. Marinate chicken breasts, turning often, for 30 minutes.

Preheat oven to 375°F. Heat the butter over medium-high heat in a heavy skillet and brown the chicken, turning once. Remove chicken from the pan and finish in the oven, approximately 15 minutes.

Warm the brandy in a small saucepan, being careful not to bring to a boil. Ignite, and quickly pour flaming brandy over chicken. Let meat rest for a couple of minutes before serving. Serve with fresh fruit salad and a dollop of chutney cream. Serves 4.

Fresh Fruit Salad:

1 iceberg lettuce, torn in bite-sized pieces
4 slices pineapple
1 cup seedless red grapes, halved
1 banana, sliced
2 tablespoons mango chutney
4 tablespoons sour cream
2-3 teaspoons curry

Prepare lettuce greens and divide amongst 4 dinner plates. Top with pineapple, red grapes and banana slices. Stir together chutney, sour cream and curry and serve as accompaniment to flambéed chicken breasts. Serves 4.

Each serving contains:

Calories	*274*	*Protein*	*22.2g*
Carbohydrates	*19.8g*	*Total fats*	*10.5g*
			(Saturated fat 4.4g)

Chicken Breast Flambé ▶

CHICKEN BREAST CHARLOTTE LANE

CHARLOTTE LANE CAFÉ & CRAFTS

Chef Roland Glauser has the ability to take ingredients not usually found together and turn them into a taste sensation. His treatment of an orange, ginger and cranberry sauce served with curry-flavoured baked chicken is easy to prepare and an elegant dinner entrée.

1 1/2-2 teaspoons curry
1/2 teaspoon paprika
1 teaspoon ground rosemary
dash of salt and pepper
4 6-ounce boneless chicken breasts
olive oil
3/4 cup fresh orange juice
2 tablespoons ginger, freshly grated
4 tablespoons honey
1 cup cranberries
1 orange, peeled, pith removed and thinly
   sliced
2 teaspoons cornstarch, dissolved in small
   amount of water

Preheat oven to 350ºF. Combine curry, paprika, rosemary, salt and pepper. Dredge chicken breasts in seasoning and arrange in a shallow baking dish. Brush breasts lightly with a small amount of olive oil and bake in oven for 30 minutes or until done.

Combine orange juice, ginger, honey and cranberries in a small saucepan. Gently heat over medium heat until cranberries are soft but not mushy. Stir in enough cornstarch mixture to create a slightly thickened sauce, add sliced orange and heat through.

Divide sauce between chicken breasts to serve. Serves 4.

Each serving contains:

Calories	*231*	*Protein*	*21.4g*
Carbohydrates	*31.0g*	*Total fats*	*2.9g*
		(Saturated fat 0.6g)	

VEAL SCALLOPPINE WITH ARTICHOKES IN A VERMOUTH SAUCE

CHEZ FRANÇOISE

One can find many variations on the classic Veal Scalloppine, yet we are sure that this creation from Chez Françoise will be a new favourite.

6 5-ounce veal cutlets
1/2 cup flour
2-3 tablespoons butter
2 cloves garlic, minced
1/4 cup dry vermouth
3/4 cup chicken broth
pinch dried marjoram
1 bay leaf
1 teaspoon lemon zest (thinly grated rind)
1 tablespoon lemon juice
6 artichoke hearts, drained and cut in quarters

Place veal between sheets of waxed paper and pound with a meat mallet until very thin, approximately 1/8-inch thick. Place flour in a shallow dish and dredge veal to lightly coat. Heat butter in a heavy bottomed skillet and sauté garlic. Add veal in batches and brown quickly on both sides. Reserve on a warm serving platter.

Deglaze skillet with vermouth and chicken broth. Stir in marjoram, bay leaf, lemon zest and juice and quartered artichokes. Boil and reduce slightly. Return veal to sauce, heat and serve immediately. Serves 6.

Each serving contains:

Calories	*360*	*Protein*	*50.2g*
Carbohydrates	*14.6g*	*Total fats*	*9.8g*
		(Saturated fat 4.2g)	

COCONUT CURRY PENNE

CHARLOTTE LANE CAFÉ & CRAFTS

This eye-catching creation from chef Roland Glauser tastes as exotic as it looks.

1 tablespoon olive oil
1 pound boneless chicken breast, sliced in thin
   strips
2 cloves garlic, finely chopped
6 cups bite-sized raw vegetables (cauliflower,
   red and green pepper, snow peas, broccoli
   etc.)
10 ounces penne pasta
1 cup heavy cream (32% m.f.)
2/3 cup grated coconut
2 teaspoons curry powder
1 teaspoon thyme
1 teaspoon rosemary
salt and pepper, to taste
1 mango, diced
fresh coriander, chopped

In a large skillet or wok, sauté sliced chicken, garlic and vegetables in olive oil. Season with spices, add coconut and cream, and simmer, covered, until vegetables are tender-crisp and chicken is cooked.

Meanwhile, cook pasta until *al dente*. Add pasta, mango and coriander to vegetable/chicken mixture, toss well and serve immediately. Serves 6.

Each serving contains:
Calories	*495*	*Protein*	*27.6g*
Carbohydrates	*53.1g*	*Total fats*	*19.7g*
		(Saturated fat 10.9g)	

VEAL ZURICH STYLE

THE WALKER INN

Theresa Walker serves this easily prepared dish with traditional Swiss Rosti potatoes and a medley of tender vegetables.

1 1/4 pounds veal cutlets
1 tablespoon vegetable oil
2 small onions, finely sliced
2 cups mushrooms, finely sliced
1 teaspoon flour
1 teaspoon rosemary, crumbled
salt and pepper, to taste
1/3 cup dry white wine
3/4 cup heavy cream

Trim veal and cut into small pieces. Heat oil in a large skillet and sauté veal a little at a time until browned on both sides. Add onion and mushrooms and sauté 2 to 3 minutes. Stir in flour and rosemary, and season with salt and pepper. Add wine and simmer 6 to 10 minutes. Stir in cream and slowly bring back to temperature, cooking until you have a creamy sauce. Serves 4.

Each serving contains:
Calories	*354*	*Protein*	*31.2g*
Carbohydrates	*4.6g*	*Total fats*	*21.0g*
		(Saturated fat 10.2g)	

GRILLED RACK OF SPRING LAMB CHOPS WITH ROSEMARY PORT DEMI-GLACE

THE ALGONQUIN HOTEL

Racks of spring lamb are available year-round in the frozen food section of most supermarkets. At the Algonquin, this dish is served with roasted garlic mashed potatoes and zucchini ribbons.

6 racks of spring lamb, 6 ribs each
6 sprigs fresh rosemary (1 teaspoon dried)
6 sprigs fresh thyme (1/2 teaspoon dry)
6 sprigs fresh oregano (1/2 teaspoon dry)
2 cloves garlic, minced
1/4 cup extra virgin olive oil
fresh rosemary sprigs, for garnish

Cut the lamb racks into 3 pieces, allowing 2 bones per chop. Combine herbs, garlic and olive oil and marinate chops, refrigerated, for 4 hours. Drain chops and grill until chops are browned on the outside and medium rare in the centre, approximately 10 to 12 minutes. Serve napped with Rosemary Port Demi-Glace and garnished with fresh rosemary. Serves 6.

Rosemary Port Demi-Glace *(recipe supplied by authors):*

The chef of the Algonquin prepares his demi-glace in the classic manner by reducing stock and espagnole, adding herbs and port. For the ease of the home cook, we are supplying a simplified version of this delightful sauce.

1 package Knorr demi-glace
1 cup cold water
1/4 cup port
2 sprigs fresh rosemary or 1 teaspoon dried, tied in a piece of cheesecloth

While chops are grilling, prepare demi-glace by adding package contents, water, port and rosemary to a small saucepan. Bring to a boil over medium-high heat, stirring frequently. Reduce heat and simmer to reduce slightly, about 10 minutes. Remove rosemary and keep warm. Yields 1 cup.

Each serving contains:

Calories	*355*	*Protein*	*20.0g*
Carbohydrates	*1.6g*	*Total fats*	*28.1g*
			(Saturated fat 11.7g)

Grilled Rack of Spring Lamb Chops with Rosemary Port Demi-Glace ▶

THAI MARINATED TENDERLOIN WITH LOBSTER SPRING ROLLS

SEASONS IN THYME

Thai cooking is relatively new to the Maritimes, and we hope you will enjoy this delicious presentation from Chef Stefan Czapalay of Seasons in Thyme.

8 ounces beef tenderloin
2 tablespoons canola oil
1 teaspoon hot chili oil
2 tablespoons minced gingerroot
1 large clove garlic, minced
2 tablespoons minced shallot
2 teaspoons brown sugar
2 teaspoons rice wine vinegar
1 tablespoon canola oil (2nd amount)
salt, for seasoning
black pepper, freshly ground, for seasoning
1 small bunch green onions, thinly sliced
1 teaspoon cornstarch
cilantro or parsley sprigs, for garnish

Slice beef into thin strips and set aside. In a small bowl, combine oils, gingerroot, garlic, shallot, sugar and vinegar. Divide marinade in half, setting half aside. Add meat to remaining marinade and refrigerate 2 to 3 hours. Remove meat and gently pat dry. Discard marinade. Mix reserved marinade with cornstarch and set aside. Preheat wok with 1 tablespoon vegetable oil over high heat, season beef with salt and pepper and sear until rare, about 30 to 40 seconds. Mix in cornstarch mixture and toss with green onions. Divide amongst 4 plates in small mounds. Serve with 2 spring rolls and garnish with sprigs of cilantro or parsley. Serves 4.

Lobster Spring Rolls:

1/2 small onion, diced
2 tablespoons canola oil
2 Savoy cabbage leaves, finely shredded
6 coriander seeds, crushed
6 Szechwan peppercorns, crushed
1 teaspoon fresh lime juice
1/2 teaspoon honey
2 tablespoons water
pinch hot red pepper sauce *or* drop of chili oil
4 ounces lobster meat, cooked and chopped
8 spring roll wrappers
1 egg white, beaten with 1 teaspoon water
2 cups peanut *or* canola oil, for deep frying (2nd amount)

In a saucepan, sweat onion in canola oil over medium heat. Add cabbage, coriander and peppercorns. Stir in lime juice, honey and 2 tablespoons water. Cover and cook over low heat until cabbage is firm but not crisp, about 10 minutes. Remove from heat and cool.

Toss lobster meat and hot red pepper or chili oil with cooled cabbage mixture. On a clean surface, lay out spring roll wrappers so that one corner points towards you. Divide cabbage and lobster mixture between wrappers, placing in centre. Brush edges of wrappers with egg wash, fold corner nearest you over filling, then fold ends in toward centre and roll into a slender cylinder. To cook, heat peanut oil to 350°F and deep fry spring rolls until golden and crisp, about 3 minutes. Remove from oil and drain on paper towelling. Yields 8 spring rolls.

Each serving contains:

Calories	470	Protein	21.9g
Carbohydrates	28.7g	Total fats	31.0g
		(Saturated fat 7.4g)	

BEEF TENDERLOIN TIPS

OFF BROADWAY CAFÉ

The beef in this recipe is cut in thin diagonal slices, which is easier to do if you partially freeze the meat first.

4 6-ounce beef tenderloins
2-3 tablespoons garlic butter
1 large onion, thinly sliced
1 medium green pepper, julienned
1 medium red pepper, julienned
3/4 pound fresh mushrooms, sliced
1/2 cup dry red wine
1 cup beef consommé
1 tablespoon cornstarch, dissolved in a little
    cold water

Cut beef in thin slices and set aside. Melt garlic butter in heavy skillet over high heat. Add beef and toss to sear. Reduce heat to medium and add vegetables, wine and consommé; stir-fry until vegetables are crisp. Stir in cornstarch dissolved in cold water, and cook until sauce is slightly thickened. Serve over steamed rice. Serves 4.

Each serving contains:
Calories	*445*	*Protein*	*24.1g*
Carbohydrates	*10.6g*	*Total fats*	*32.3g*
		(Saturated fat 14.2g)	

BAKED HAM WITH RHUBARB RELISH

STEAMERS STOP INN

Pat Stewart of Steamers Stop Inn prepares several bottles of this relish when the rhubarb first appears in the spring. She tells us it is delicious served with roasted pork or ham.

Relish:

4 cups rhubarb, diced
4 cups onions, finely chopped
1 1/2 cups white vinegar
3 cups brown sugar
1 teaspoon salt
1 teaspoon pepper
1 teaspoon whole cloves
1 teaspoon whole allspice

Combine rhubarb, onion and vinegar in a large kettle and bring to a boil. Immediately reduce heat and simmer 30 minutes, stirring occasionally. Add sugar, salt and pepper. Tie cloves and allspice in a cheesecloth bag and add to other ingredients. Cook over medium heat for an additional 30 minutes. Bottle immediately in sterilized jars and store in a cool, dark cupboard. Yields 4 to 5 8-ounce jars.

Baked Ham (recipe supplied by authors):

1/2 uncooked ham (approximately 6-8
    pounds)
1 tablespoon whole cloves

Preheat oven to 325°F. Score ham fat about 1/4 inch deep and stud with whole cloves. Place on a rack and bake approximately 25 minutes per pound or until a meat thermometer indicates an internal temperature of 160°F. Slice and serve accompanied by Rhubarb Relish. Serves 6 to 8.

Each 5 oz. meat serving contains:
Calories	*304*	*Protein*	*27.8g*
Carbohydrates	*6.4g*	*Total fats*	*17.7g*
		(Saturated fat 6.3g)	

SPINACH STUFFED PORK TENDERLOIN

THE LION INN

This is an elegant dish, suitable for a grand dinner party. It can be prepared in advance, allowing the hostess time to spend with her guests. Simply place it in the oven an hour before serving time.

2 12-ounce pork tenderloins,
6 ounces fresh spinach, washed and dried
1 medium onion, finely chopped
1 small clove garlic, minced (optional)
1 tablespoon butter
1/4 cup ricotta cheese
2 tablespoons toasted almonds
salt and pepper, to taste
1 1/2 tablespoons Dijon mustard
4 slices lean bacon

Preheat oven to 350°F. Remove excess fat and silver skin from tenderloin. Butterfly tenderloin and flatten gently with a meat mallet, being careful not to split meat.

Steam spinach until wilted and drain well to remove excess moisture. Sweat onion and garlic in butter until softened, about 5 minutes. Add cooked spinach to onion mixture and chop fairly fine. Set aside to cool. Add ricotta and almonds; season with salt and pepper, and mix lightly. Spread Dijon mustard over cut sides of tenderloins, top with spinach mixture and roll up as tightly as possible without squeezing out the stuffing. Wrap with bacon and secure with a toothpick.

Place tenderloins, cut side down, in a roasting pan. Each tenderloin should be touching its neighbour. Bake 45 minutes to 1 hour. Remove from oven, tent with foil and let rest 10 minutes. Serve, sliced in rounds and napped with Brown Sauce Gravy. Serves 4 to 6.

Brown Sauce Gravy:

1 1/2 tablespoons pan drippings or butter
3/4 cup beef broth
1/4 cup dry red wine
1/2 bay leaf
1/2 teaspoon parsley
1 tablespoon butter
1 1/2 tablespoons flour

Combine drippings and butter in roasting pan. Add broth and wine and bring to a boil. Add bay leaf and parsley and boil briskly until liquid is reduced by 1/3. Knead together butter and flour. Form into small balls and add to boiling sauce, one at a time, stirring constantly, until sauce reaches the consistency of heavy cream. Discard bay leaf and serve. Yields 3/4 cup.

Each serving contains:

Calories	*354*	*Protein*	*18.7g*
Carbohydrates	*5.0g*	*Total fats*	*29.4g*
		(Saturated fat 11.9g)	

THYME ROAST PORK LOIN WITH BOURBON SAUCE

THE INN AT BAY FORTUNE

Ask your butcher to trim all excess fat from the loin of pork roast. Chef Michael Smith serves his dish with the Cranberry Turnip Tart on page 100 and a bourbon sauce.

2 pounds boneless loin roast of pork
6-8 slices lean bacon
1 tablespoon fresh thyme, minced (1 teaspoon dried)
salt and pepper, to season
Bourbon Sauce (recipe follows)

Preheat oven to 300°F. Allow bacon to come to room temperature. Rub thyme, salt and pepper all over the pork loin. Tightly wrap loin with bacon, slightly overlapping each slice.

Place roast in oven and bake 30 minutes. Turn oven to 450°F and continue roasting until bacon is crisp, meat is slightly pink in the center and a meat thermometer registers 160F. Remove to a platter, tent with foil and let stand 10 minutes. Slice pork and serve with Bourbon Sauce. Serves 4 to 6.

Bourbon Sauce:

1 1/2 teaspoons olive oil
1 small onion, sliced
1/2 medium carrot, diced
1/2 teaspoon minced garlic
2 cups chicken broth
dash allspice
salt and pepper, to taste
1/4 cup bourbon

Sweat onions and carrots over medium heat in olive oil until caramelized, stirring often. Add garlic and sweat 1 additional minute. Add broth and allspice and simmer until liquid reduces by 1/2. Purée thoroughly in a blender. Season with salt and pepper, add bourbon and reheat. Yields 1 cup.

Each serving contains:
Calories	*230*	*Protein*	*10*
Carbohydrates	*20*	*Total fats*	*3g*

Thyme Roast Pork Loin with Bourbon Sauce ▶

VEGETABLES

Vegetables offer our Maritime chefs an opportunity to set the mood for their creations. We feel certain that after you see the photographs on these pages, you will agree that Maritime vegetable dishes can be elegant and imaginative.

We particularly enjoyed the recipe for spaghetti squash from The Marshlands Inn in Sackville. We also recommend Cooper's Inn Vegetables for food that is unadorned, crisp and full of natural flavour, while the Baked Acorn Squash with Sherry from The Doctor's Inn is colourful, easily prepared and delicious.

◄ *Asparagus & Roast Tomato Risotto with Watercress*

ASPARAGUS & ROAST TOMATO RISOTTO WITH WATERCRESS

INN AT BAY FORTUNE

Italian arborio rice with its rounded grains has a capacity to hold its shape and remain firm during cooking. Remove from heat while the rice is still fairly firm to the bite (al dente), *as rice will continue to cook as long as it is hot.*

3 1/2 to 4 1/2 cups celery juice*
4 tomatoes
1/2 cup olive oil
1 teaspoon salt
1/2 teaspoon pepper, freshly ground
1 3/4 cups arborio rice
1 teaspoon garlic, minced
1/2 cup white wine
3 cups asparagus, cut in 1/2-inch pieces
3/4 cup Parmesan-Reggiano cheese, grated
watercress, chopped

Preheat oven to 500°F. Bring celery juice to simmer in a saucepan. Cut tomatoes into wedges and toss with 1/4 cup of the olive oil. Arrange tomatoes on a baking sheet, sprinkle with salt and pepper and bake for 15 minutes until they "roast."

In a heavy-bottomed saucepan, heat the remaining oil over medium heat. Add the rice and garlic and stir until the rice is evenly coated and begins to feel "chalky," approximately 6 to 8 minutes. Add wine and stir until it is absorbed.

Add the boiling juice, a ladleful at a time, stirring to assist the absorption process. Continue adding liquid until 1/3 of the juice remains. Add asparagus and continue cooking and adding liquid until rice is slightly *al dente*. Turn off heat, stir in cheese and watercress and serve immediately with the roasted tomatoes. Serves 4.

*If celery juice is not commercially available, you can prepare celery broth. Wash, separate and chop one bunch of celery. Boil in 5 cups of water until celery is cooked. Purée in a food processor and strain through a fine sieve. Return to saucepan and reduce to 4 1/2 cups. You may also substitute vegetable stock for the juice in the recipe.

Each serving contains:

Calories	*418*	*Protein*	*11.2g*
Carbohydrates	*56.3g*	*Total fats*	*15.6g*
		(Saturated fat 3.6g)	

JEAN OFFER'S ZUCCHINI WEDGES

THE DOCTOR'S INN

Innkeeper Jean Offer grows fresh herbs in the garden at The Doctor's Inn, so she often uses one tablespoon of fresh basil in place of the dried basil listed in the recipe.

1/2 teaspoon butter
3 small zucchinis, thinly sliced
1 large onion, thinly sliced
4 ounces Cheddar cheese, grated
1 large tomato, sliced
salt and pepper, to taste
1 teaspoon dried basil

Butter the bottom of a 10-inch skillet. Arrange zucchini slices over bottom of skillet and partially up the sides. Top with onion and half of the cheese. Repeat with another layer of zucchini, onion and cheese. Top with tomato and season with salt, pepper and basil. Cover skillet and simmer over low to medium heat on the top of the stove. When vegetables are fork tender, about 20 minutes, cut in wedges and serve. Serves 6.

Each serving contains:
Calories	97	Protein	5.9g
Carbohydrates	4.1g	Total fats	6.8g
		(Saturated fat 4.2g)	

BAKED ACORN SQUASH WITH SHERRY

THE DOCTOR'S INN

"Pick and serve," is the motto of Paul and Jean Offer when they serve dinner to guests in the dining room of their small inn in rural Prince Edward Island. This dish lends itself well to their philosophy.

2 small acorn squash
2 tablespoons butter, melted
1/4 cup brown sugar
2 tablespoons sherry

Preheat oven to 350°F. Rinse and pat dry squash, trim tops and ends, cut in 1/2 around the centre and scoop out seeds. Slice squash into rounds and place in a greased baking dish. Brush squash slices with melted butter and bake until tender, 25 to 30 minutes. Remove from oven, sprinkle with brown sugar and drizzle with sherry. Return to oven and bake an additional 5 minutes. Serves 6 to 8.

Each serving contains:
Calories	90	Protein	0.9g
Carbohydrates	15.8g	Total fats	3.0g
		(Saturated fat 1.8g)	

CRANBERRY STUFFING

WHITE POINT BEACH LODGE &
RESORT

*This colourful dressing is an ideal accompaniment
to roasted poultry or pork. Simply place in the oven
during the last half hour of roasting time.*

2 cloves garlic, crushed
2 green onions, chopped
1 stalk celery, chopped
1 small carrot, finely diced
1 tablespoon oil
1/4 teaspoon white pepper
1/2 teaspoon salt
1 loaf French style bread, cut in small cubes
1 cup fresh cranberries
2 teaspoons fresh mint, finely chopped (1/2
  teaspoon dried)
2 cups apple juice

Preheat oven to 350°F. Sauté garlic, onions,
celery and carrot in oil over medium heat for
3 to 5 minutes. Season with pepper and salt.
Combine vegetables with bread cubes,
cranberries, mint and apple juice. Place in
lightly greased loaf pan and cover with foil.
Bake 30 minutes, loosen sides and invert onto
a serving platter. Serve in slices. Serves 6 to 8.

Each serving contains:

Calories	*223*	*Protein*	*6.0g*
Carbohydrates	*42.3g*	*Total fats*	*3.6g*
		(Saturated fat 0.6g)	

LITTLE SHEMOGUE BAKED SQUASH

LITTLE SHEMOGUE COUNTRY INN

*This is an excellent dish to prepare and bake with
roast beef or turkey. If you are using a lower oven
temperature for your meat, simply bake a little
longer.*

4 cups buttercup squash, peeled and cut in 3/4
  inch cubes
1 1/2 cups orange juice
1 teaspoon brown sugar
1/8 teaspoon nutmeg
salt and pepper, to taste
2 tablespoons butter

Preheat oven to 350°F. Place squash in a
buttered, shallow casserole. Mix together
orange juice, brown sugar, nutmeg, salt and
pepper and pour over squash. Dot with butter
and bake until squash cubes are tender,
approximately 35 to 45 minutes. Serves 4 to 6.

Each serving contains:

Calories	*81*	*Protein*	*1.5g*
Carbohydrates	*10.1g*	*Total fats*	*4.1g*
		(Saturated fat 2.4g)	

Little Shemogue Baked Squash ▶

SPAGHETTI SQUASH

THE MARSHLANDS INN

Spaghetti squash is a member of the summer squash family, and this innovative vegetable is finding its way into Maritime kitchens and hearts.

1 medium (2 1/2 -3 pound) spaghetti squash
1/2 cup butter, softened
3 tablespoons brown sugar
1/4 teaspoon cinnamon
1/4 teaspoon allspice
1/4 teaspoon nutmeg

Preheat oven to 350ºF. Cut the squash in half lengthwise, scoop out and discard seeds. Pierce squash skin with the tines of a fork, place cut side down on a cookie sheet and bake until the skin is soft and the squash is tender, about 45 minutes.

Combine softened butter, brown sugar, cinnamon, allspice and nutmeg in a large bowl. Using a fork, remove the pulp from the shell (it will look like "spaghetti"). Add to the butter mixture and toss with 2 forks to coat. Serves 4 to 6.

Each serving contains:

Calories	*157*	*Protein*	*0.3g*
Carbohydrates	*5.8g*	*Total fats*	*13.3g*
		(Saturated fat 9.5g)	

THE PINES RICE PILAF

THE PINES RESORT HOTEL

The chefs at The Pines tell us that this is an excellent dish to make ahead. To reheat, simply place in a buttered gratin dish, cover with foil and bake at 350ºF until hot, approximately 20 minutes.

1 tablespoon olive oil
1 clove garlic, minced
1/2 red pepper, finely chopped
1/2 teaspoon ground cumin
1 teaspoon salt
pepper, freshly ground
1/2 cinnamon stick
1 1/2 cups long grain rice, rinsed with cold water
3 cups boiling water
2 tablespoons fresh coriander or parsley, chopped

Heat oil in a large saucepan over medium heat. Add garlic and peppers and sauté for 3 minutes or until peppers soften. Stir in cumin, cinnamon stick, salt, pepper and rice. Add boiling water, reduce heat to minimum, cover and simmer until rice is tender and liquid is absorbed, approximately 20 minutes. Remove from heat and let stand, covered, for 5 minutes. Remove cinammon stick and stir in coriander or parsley. Serves 6.

Each serving contains:

Calories	*150*	*Protein*	*2.2g*
Carbohydrates	*31.9g*	*Total fats*	*2.4g*
		(Saturated fat 0.3g)	

Spaghetti Squash ▶

92

COOPER'S INN VEGETABLES

COOPER'S INN & RESTAURANT

Cooper's Inn prides itself upon serving the freshest of vegetables. Blanching fixes the colour of the vegetables, preserving the natural sugars and saving the vitamins. The cooks at Cooper's tell us that the "carrots should be slightly firm in the centre and the beans should squeak on your teeth."

2 long, fat carrots, peeled and sliced into 3-inch sticks
1/2 small turnip, peeled and cut into 1/2-inch squares
1 small cauliflower, separated into florets
1 small bunch broccoli, separated into florets
1/2 pound green and yellow beans, trimmed
2-3 tablespoons Pesto Sauce (see recipe page 61)

Wash and carefully prepare vegetables. Bring a large pot of unsalted water to a rolling boil over high heat. Add carrots and turnip and cook 1 minute; add cauliflower and broccoli and cook 2 minutes longer. Add beans and cook an additional 2 minutes (total cooking time is 5 minutes). Drain vegetables and toss with pesto, if desired. Serves 6.

Each serving contains:
Calories	*73*	*Protein*	*4.7g*
Carbohydrates	*10.6g*	*Total fats*	*2.7g*
			(Saturated fat 0.7g)

ROASTED RED POTATOES, RUTABAGA & SQUASH

DUNCREIGAN COUNTRY INN

At Duncreigan, Eleanor Mullendore serves dishes that are innovative yet traditional, and influenced by the good things Cape Breton has to offer.

1/4 cup olive oil
1/4 cup butter
2 cloves garlic, minced
1/2 teaspoon red pepper flakes
1 tablespoon paprika
1 teaspoon dried rosemary, crushed
salt and pepper, to taste
4-6 red potatoes, scrubbed, quartered and left unpeeled
1 small squash, peeled and cut into 2-inch cubes
1 small rutabaga, peeled and cut into 2-inch cubes

In a small saucepan over medium heat, combine first 7 ingredients and stir until butter is melted. Remove from burner and cool 2 hours, allowing flavours to develop.

Preheat oven to 400°F. Prepare vegetables and place on a lightly greased baking sheet. Brush vegetables with marinade and bake 10 minutes. Brush again with marinade and continue baking until vegetables are crisp on the outside and tender inside, approximately 30 minutes. Serves 4 to 6.

Each serving contains:
Calories	*165*	*Protein*	*2.8g*
Carbohydrates	*20.7g*	*Total fats*	*8.7g*
			(Saturated fat 3.0g)

FRIED GREEN TOMATOES

QUARTERDECK BEACHSIDE VILLAS & GRILL

Everyone who loved the movie will surely love this rendition of Fried Green Tomatoes. Chefs Derek Gillespie and Jane-Marie Cameron serve this vegetable with a variety of entrées.

6 green tomatoes
3 tablespoons flour
1 teaspoon salt
pepper, to taste
1 teaspoon sugar
4 slices bacon, chopped

Wash tomatoes, remove stem ends and slice in 1/4-inch rounds. Mix flour, salt, pepper and sugar together in a small bowl. Coat tomato slices and reserve. Heat a skillet over medium heat, add chopped bacon and, when crispy, add tomato slices. Brown on both sides. Serves 6 to 8.

Each serving contains:

Calories	68	*Protein*	3.0g
Carbohydrates	9.0g	*Total fats*	2.4g
		(Saturated fat 0.8g)	

VEGETABLE RIBBON STIR FRY

THE SHADOW LAWN INN

The chef at The Shadow Lawn Inn likes to serve seasonal vegetables with a crisp-tender texture. This healthy vegetable presentation is best made just minutes before serving.

1/2 medium turnip, peeled
2 carrots, peeled
2 small zucchinis
2 small yellow summer squash
pinch salt, pepper, oregano and basil
1 tablespoon olive oil

Using a carrot peeler, shave vegetables into long ribbon strips. In a skillet, heat oil over medium-high heat and sauté turnip and carrot strips for 1 1/2 minutes, tossing gently. Add zucchini and summer squash, season with salt, pepper and herbs and continue to sauté for an additional 1 1/2 minutes. Serve immediately. Serves 4.

Each serving contains:

Calories	72	*Protein*	2.0g
Carbohydrates	9.3g	*Total fats*	3.7g
		(Saturated fat 0.5g)	

GREEN BEAN, ZUCCHINI & POTATO STEW

THE MARSHLANDS INN

At The Marshlands Inn, the chef serves this delicious stew in bowls topped with small chunks of feta cheese and accompanied by crusty bread.

1/4 cup extra virgin olive oil
1 cup onion, diced
1 pound green beans, trimmed and halved
generous dash cayenne pepper, or to taste
1 small zucchini, in thick slices
2 medium russet potatoes, peeled and cubed
5 large sprigs fresh parsley, chopped
1 28-ounce can Italian-style tomatoes
salt and pepper, to taste

Heat oil in a large skillet over medium-high heat. Add onion and sauté 3 minutes, stirring often. Add green beans and cayenne and sauté until onion is translucent, about 3 minutes. Stir in zucchini, potato and parsley. Drain tomatoes, reserving their juices. Chop tomatoes and add, with juice, to skillet. Season with salt and pepper, cover and reduce heat. Cook at a simmer until vegetables are tender, approximately 45 minutes. Serves 4 to 6.

Each serving contains:

Calories	168	Protein	3.8g
Carbohydrates	20.0g	Total fats	9.6g
		(Saturated fat 1.3g)	

KELTIC LODGE'S GRILLED VEGETABLES

KELTIC LODGE

The chef at Keltic Lodge serves these vegetables with his Grilled Atlantic Salmon Fillets. He suggests you place the vegetable packet on the grill about 5 minutes before grilling the salmon.

1 cup snow peas, ends and strings removed
1-2 large tomatoes, thickly sliced
1 cup mushrooms, quartered
1 green pepper, julienned
1 red pepper, julienned
1 clove garlic, minced
3 green onions, thinly sliced
2 teaspoons butter
salt and pepper, to taste

Prepare vegetables and place on a large piece of aluminum foil, dot with butter and season with salt and pepper. Fold foil into a packet, allowing a little space for steam to expand, but making sure that the edges are well sealed. Place vegetables on a hot grill and cook until vegetables are crisp tender, approximately 12 to 15 minutes. Turn once during cooking. Serves 4.

Each serving contains:

Calories	91	Protein	4.3g
Carbohydrates	15.9g	Total fats	2.5g
		(Saturated fat 1.3g)	

Green Bean, Zucchini & Potato Stew ▶

STIR FRY SQUASH WITH SPICY VINAIGRETTE

THE MARSHLANDS INN

This is an ideal dish to serve when zucchini and yellow squash are abundant in your garden.

3 medium zucchini squash
3 medium yellow squash
1 tablespoon vegetable oil
1 tablespoon gingerroot, peeled and minced
2 tablespoons Chinese rice wine or sake
3 tablespoons fresh coriander, chopped
Vinaigrette (recipe follows)

Trim ends from squash and halve lengthwise. Cut each half crosswise into 3-inch sections and slice in to 1/4-inch strips. Heat oil in a wok and sauté ginger until tender. Add squashes and wine and stir fry 5 minutes until crisp-tender. Stir in wine and coriander and bring to serving temperature. To serve, toss with warm Vinaigrette (recipe follows). Serves 4 to 6.

Vinaigrette:

2 tablespoons dark sesame oil
1 teaspoon dried hot red pepper flakes (or to taste)
1/4 cup soya sauce
3 tablespoons unflavoured rice wine vinegar
1 tablespoon sugar
salt, to taste

Heat oil in a small saucepan until it starts to smoke. Add pepper flakes. Cover and remove from burner. Let stand 3 minutes. Stir in remaining vinaigrette ingredients, stirring until sugar is dissolved. Toss with warm zucchini. Yields 1/4 cup.

Each serving contains:

Calories	*102*	*Protein*	*2.2g*
Carbohydrates	*8.5g*	*Total fats*	*7.1g*
			(Saturated fat 1.0g)

COUNTRY MASH

SEASONS IN THYME

Chef Stefan Czapalay's Country Mash is a restaurant favourite during the autumn and early winter season. We feel it is a nice accompaniment for seafood, poultry or beef.

4 medium to large Yukon Gold potatoes,
   peeled and quartered
2 cloves garlic
1/2 medium parsnip, peeled and sliced
1/4 pound buttercup squash, peeled and
   cubed
2 tablespoons butter
salt and pepper, to taste

Cook potatoes, garlic, parsnip and squash in a small amount of water until fork tender. Drain, add butter, season with salt and pepper and mash. Serves 4.

Each serving contains:

Calories	*159*	*Protein*	*3.0g*
Carbohydrates	*24.9g*	*Total fats*	*5.9g*
		(Saturated fat 3.6g)	

CRANBERRY TURNIP TART

INN AT BAY FORTUNE

If you are fortunate enough to own a mandoline, simply slice your turnip into uniform slices. Chef Michael Smith tells us that this is an excellent "make ahead" dish, because it can be chilled, then cut into wedges and reheated in a microwave.

1 large turnip, peeled
1 cup dried cranberries
1 small onion, finely diced
salt and pepper, to taste

Preheat oven to 350°F. Thinly slice the turnip into 1/4-inch slices. Line the bottom of a baking pan with waxed paper and oil the entire pan. Fit the turnip into the pan in layers, sprinkling each layer with onion, cranberries, salt and pepper. Your final layer should be turnip. Cover the pan tightly with foil and poke 2 small holes in the covering to allow steam to escape. Bake 2 hours or until a skewer can be easily inserted through the layers.

Remove from oven, cut around the outside edge of baking dish and allow vegetables to rest 30 minutes. Invert onto a serving plate and reheat briefly before serving. Serves 6.

Each serving contains:

Calories	*22*	*Protein*	*0.5g*
Carbohydrates	*5.4g*	*Total fats*	*0.1g*
		(Saturated fat 0.0g)	

(See photo page 84.)

BREADED PUMPKIN SLICES WITH TOMATO SAUCE

THE SALMON RIVER HOUSE INN

*This is an easy vegetable casserole to accompany almost any main dish,
especially grilled seafood and meat.*

1 small pie pumpkin (approximately 2
   pounds), peeled, seeded and sliced
2 eggs, beaten
3/4 cup dry breadcrumbs
1/2 cup butter, melted
Tomato Sauce (recipe follows)
1/4 cup Parmesan cheese, grated

Preheat oven to 350°F. Dip pumpkin slices in egg and coat with breadcrumbs. Heat butter in a skillet and saute pumpkin slices in batches, browning on all sides. Transfer pumpkin to an overproof baking dish, cover with Tomato Sauce and sprinkle with Parmesan cheese. Bake 30 minutes until sauce is bubbly and pumpkin is tender. Serves 6 to 8.

Tomato Sauce:

2 tablespoons olive oil
1 onion, finely chopped
1 clove garlic, crushed
4 medium tomatoes, peeled, seeded and
   chopped
1 tablespoon tomato paste
1 teaspoon basil
1 tablespoon parsley, chopped
1 teaspoon sugar
salt and pepper, to taste

Heat olive oil in a saucepan over medium heat, add onion and garlic and sauté until onion is soft but not browned. Stir in remaining ingredients and simmer 10 minutes. Yields 1 cup.

Each serving contains:

Calories	*236*	*Protein*	*4.9g*
Carbohydrates	*18.0g*	*Total fats*	*17.2g*
			(Saturated fat 8.4g)

DESSERTS

For some, the dessert makes the dinner, while others are looking for something just a wee bit sweet, but not too filling, with which to complete their meal. In an effort to satisfy everyone, we have offered in this collection several lighter choices such as Pears on a Cloud from West Point Light House, or Compass Rose's Seasonal Fruit with Maple Cream. For those of you with an exceptional craving for something totally decadent, we have included Chocolate Overdose Cheesecake from the Off Broadway Café, and Egg Nog Ice Cream in Caramel Cages from Seasons in Thyme. Enjoy!

◄ *Harvest Pumpkin Soufflé*

HARVEST PUMPKIN SOUFFLÉ

TATTINGSTONE INN

Catherine Metzger, daughter of innkeeper Betsey Harwood, developed this delicious recipe for the inn's menu. With its spicy flavour and light texture it is a welcome alternative to the traditional harvest-time pumpkin pie.

3 eggs, at room temperature
1 1/2 cup pumpkin, cooked and puréed
1 cup light brown sugar, packed
1/2 cup whole milk
3/4 teaspoon cinnamon
1/8 teaspoon ground ginger
3/4 teaspoon allspice
1/2 teaspoon nutmeg
1/2 teaspoon salt
1 envelope unflavoured gelatin
1/4 cup warm water
1/2 cup pecans, ground, for garnish

Prepare a 3-cup soufflé dish by securely tying a waxed paper collar around the edge, extending at least 4 inches above the rim.

Separate eggs. Beat yolks and reserve whites. Combine pumpkin, brown sugar, milk, ginger, cinnamon, nutmeg, allspice and salt in a saucepan. Cook pumpkin mixture over medium heat, stirring gently until first bubbles appear and it begins to boil. Remove from heat and whisk in egg yolks. Set aside.

Soften gelatin in warm water until completely dissolved, approximately 3 minutes. Whisk gelatin into the pumpkin mixture until smooth and creamy. Refrigerate until it starts to set, approximately 40 minutes.

Beat egg whites until soft peaks form. Fold pumpkin mixture into the egg whites, 1/3 at a time, until completely combined. Pour into the soufflé dish, smooth top and refrigerate 6 to 8 hours. To serve, remove collar and gently press pecans into the sides of the soufflé. Serves 6.

Each serving contains:

Calories	*221*	*Protein*	*5.2g*
Carbohydrates	*31.4g*	*Total fats*	*9.5g*
			(Saturated fat 1.8g)

PEARS ON A CLOUD

WEST POINT LIGHTHOUSE

Carol Livingstone of West Point Lighthouse tells us that when customers are looking for something light after dinner, she prepares this colourful dessert using either apricot or orange jello powder.

1 15-ounce can Bartlett pear halves, packed in their own juice
1 3-ounce package orange or apricot Jello
1 cup boiling water
1 teaspoon powdered gelatin
1/4 cup cold water
2/3 cup pear juice
1 tablespoon lemon juice
1 package Dream Whip
1/2 cup 2% milk
1/2 teaspoon vanilla
fresh mint leaves, for garnish

Drain pears, reserving liquid. Combine Jello powder and boiling water, stirring until fully dissolved. Dissolve unflavoured gelatin in cold water, allowing to stand 5 minutes. Stir unflavoured gelatin into Jello mixture and add reserved pear juice. Cool in refrigerator until partially set, approximately 1 1/2 hours.

Remove mixture from refrigerator and beat with an electric mixer until foamy. Prepare Dream Whip with cold milk, following package directions. Stir in vanilla. Fold gelatin mixture into Dream Whip mixture and spoon into individual dessert dishes. Chill until set. At serving time, gently slice pears and fan three slices on top of desserts. Garnish with fresh mint leaves, if desired. Serves 6 to 8.

Each serving contains:

Calories	*116*	*Protein*	*5.2g*
Carbohydrates	*31.4g*	*Total fats*	*2.9g*
		(Saturated fat 2.3g)	

TATTINGSTONE INN CHOCOLATE PÂTÉ

TATTINGSTONE INN

We never like to ask for an inn's hallmark recipe, but innkeeper Betsey Harwood has agreed to share her Chocolate Pâté with us. She stresses the importance of using high-quality chocolate in its preparation.

10 ounces bittersweet chocolate
1 cup heavy cream (32% m.f.)
Crème Anglaise (recipe follows)
2 cups fresh raspberries
mint leaves, for garnish

Chop chocolate and set in a heatproof bowl over hot, but not boiling, water. Stir chocolate with cream until melted. Pour into a bowl and cover with plastic wrap directly on the chocolate surface. Refrigerate overnight until firm. To serve, ladle 1/4 cup Crème Anglaise onto serving plates. Place a small scoop of pâté on the cream sauce and garnish with fresh raspberries and mint leaves. Serves 8.

Crème Anglaise:

2 cups heavy cream (32% m.f.)
4 egg yolks
2/3 cup sugar

Heat cream in the top of a double boiler over hot, but not boiling, water. Whisk together yolks and sugar, until they are light yellow in colour. Stir a small amount of the hot mixture into the yolks. Return yolks to hot mixture and cook gently until mixture lightly coats the back of a spoon, approximately 6 to 10 minutes. Strain through a fine sieve into a bowl, place a layer of plastic wrap directly upon the surface and refrigerate. Yields 2 cups.

Each serving contains:
Calories	540	Protein	5.1g
Carbohydrates	45.5g	Total fats	41.0g
		(Saturated fat	24.4g)

CHOCOLATE OVERDOSE CHEESECAKE

OFF BROADWAY CAFÉ

This recipe is for the true chocoholic who searches the dessert menu for the sweet with the most chocolate content. We recommend this dessert for special occasions. Be advised that a small sliver will satisfy the sweetest tooth.

2 1/2 cups shortbread cookie crumbs
2 ounces semi-sweet chocolate, melted
3 tablespoons butter, melted
1 1/2 pounds cream cheese, at room
 temperature (tested using low-fat)
4 eggs
1 can (300 ml) sweetened condensed milk
 (tested using "lite")
8 ounces semi-sweet chocolate, melted
 (second amount)
1 teaspoon vanilla
2 1/2 ounces semi-sweet chocolate, melted
 (third amount)
1/4 cup butter, melted (second amount)

Preheat oven to 300°F. Combine cookie crumbs, melted chocolate and butter, and press into bottom of a 9-inch springform pan. Beat cream cheese until soft. Add eggs, condensed milk, chocolate (second amount) and vanilla and beat until smooth. Pour cheese mixture over crumb base and bake for 1 to 1 1/4 hours, until cooked. Remove from oven.

Blend together third amount of chocolate and second amount of butter and spread over top of warm cheesecake. Chill 4 to 5 hours before serving. Serves 12 to 16.

Each serving contains:
Calories	513	Protein	10.8g
Carbohydrates	51.4g	Total fats	30.9g
		(Saturated fat	15.4g)

Tattingstone Inn Chocolate Pâté ▶

SEASONAL FRUIT WITH MAPLE CREAM

COMPASS ROSE INN

Rodger Pike of the Compass Rose Inn uses this recipe throughout the seasons. We tested it using banana slices and orange segments and found it delightful.

1 cup low-fat sour cream
1/4 cup maple syrup
2 tablespoons brandy
3 cups fresh fruit

In a bowl, whisk together the sour cream, maple syrup and brandy. Refrigerate. Serve drizzled over fresh fruit. Yields 1 1/4 cups and serves 6.

Each serving contains:
Calories	*81*	*Protein*	*1.2g*
Carbohydrates	*14.8g*	*Total fats*	*1.1g*
		(Saturated fat	*0.0g)*

PEPPERED STRAWBERRIES WITH A WARM ZABAGLIONE SAUCE

SUNSHINE CAFÉ

It may seem strange to add pepper to fresh strawberries, but it does heighten the flavour and creates a wonderful dessert.

2 cups fresh strawberries, cut in halves or quarters
1-2 tablespoons Grand Marnier liqueur
2 tablespoons sugar (less if berries are very sweet)
4 good turns of a pepper mill
Zabaglione Sauce (recipe follows)
vanilla ice-cream

Prepare strawberries and place in a bowl. Add Grand Marnier, sugar and pepper and toss to combine. Refrigerate while making Zabaglione Sauce.

To serve, place a small scoop of vanilla ice-cream in a parfait glass. Top ice-cream with peppered strawberries, drizzle with Zabaglione Sauce and serve immediately. Serves 4 to 6.

Zabaglione Sauce:

4 egg yolks
1/3 cup sugar
1/2 cup Marsala wine or sweet white wine

Whisk together egg yolks, sugar and wine and continue beating for 1 minute, until well combined. Put yolk mixture in top of a double boiler over simmering water. Continue whisking, being careful not to curdle eggs, until sauce is very creamy and very warm, approximately 10 minutes. Yields 2/3 cup.

Each serving contains:
Calories	*278*	*Protein*	*6.8g*
Carbohydrates	*35.8g*	*Total fats*	*10.8g*
		(Saturated fat	*5.5g)*

TIDE'S TABLE SEAWEED PIE

INN ON THE COVE

Ross Mavis likes to serve this pie to visitors from away. After they tell him how much they enjoyed their dessert, he tells them that it is "Seaweed Pie." He notes that both Irish moss and dulse are readily available in health food stores.

1 9-inch pastry or crumb pie shell, baked
1 cup Irish moss (carrageen), thoroughly
   washed in cold water
3 1/2 cups milk
1 cup sugar
pinch of salt
1/4 cup fresh berries (raspberries or
   blueberries)
1 tablespoon sugar (second amount)
1 tablespoon cornstarch
dulse flakes and fresh berries, for garnish

Coarsely chop prepared moss and place in a cheesecloth bag, tying well with a string. Pour milk into a heavy bottomed saucepan, add moss bag and heat gently over low heat, stirring frequently. As milk warms, squeeze bag with a wooden spoon to help extract thickener. Continue squeezing bag with spoon while heating milk for about 20 to 30 minutes. Do not allow milk to boil. Remove pan from heat and discard bag. Add sugar and pinch of salt, stir to dissolve and let mixture cool.

Heat 1/4 cup fruit in small saucepan with sugar and cornstarch. Crush fruit with a spoon, stir well and heat until sugar dissolves and mixture is bubbling. Remove from heat and let cool slightly. Add fruit to cooled milk mixture, stirring to combine. When quite cool and thickened, spoon into prepared pie shell and chill in refrigerator until firm. Garnish with fresh berries and a light dusting of dulse flakes. Serves 8.

Each serving contains:
Calories	230	*Protein*	5.3g
Carbohydrates	32.1g	*Total fats*	9.6g
		(Saturated fat 2.8g)	

POACHED PEARS IN RED WINE

SEASONS IN THYME

Chef Stefan Czapalay tells us that Zinfandel wine works very well in this recipe. He cautions that for best results, you should refrigerate the pears overnight before serving.

2 cups fruity red wine
5 peppercorns
5 whole cloves
1 cinnamon stick
2 tablespoons brown sugar
2 tablespoons honey
1/2 teaspoon nutmeg
4 pears, peeled with stems

Combine the wine, spices, sugar and honey in a saucepan and bring to a simmer. Carefully peel pears, leaving stems intact. Place pears in liquid, cover and gently poach until just tender, approximately 18 to 20 minutes. Allow pears to cool in liquid, then refrigerate overnight. Serves 4.

Each serving contains:
Calories	168	*Protein*	0.7g
Carbohydrates	38.7g	*Total fats*	0.7g

(See photo page 117.)

APPLE ACADIAN

THE PANSY PATCH

This dessert appeals to the palate by managing to be both tart and sweet. At The Pansy Patch, it is served with a rich vanilla sauce. In keeping with the lighter theme of this book, we have taken the liberty of including a Crème Anglaise recipe as well.

6 baking apples (approximately 2 1/2 inches in diameter)
1 cup cranberry sauce
4 sheets phyllo pastry
1/4 cup butter, melted
Vanilla Sauce *or* Crème Anglaise

Preheat oven to 375°F. Core the apples and score the skin around them. Loosely fill apple cavities with cranberry sauce. Brush sheets of phyllo pastry with melted butter, then cut into 6 equal squares. Place one apple on a phyllo square and fold the pastry up and around the apple. Turn the apple upside down and place the second square of pastry on and around the apple. Return apple to its upright position and place on remaining 2 squares of pastry; fold pastry corner-to-corner and twist the top to seal. Repeat procedure with remaining apples.

Place apples on ungreased baking sheet and bake for 20 to 30 minutes (length of time will depend upon type of apple used). Test for doneness with a toothpick: if toothpick goes in smoothly, apple is cooked. To serve, place apple on a dessert plate garnished with Vanilla Sauce or Crème Anglaise. Serves 6.

Vanilla Sauce:

1 cup heavy cream (35% m.f.)
1/2 cup icing sugar, sifted
1/2 teaspoon vanilla
1 tablespoon cornstarch, mixed with small amount of cold water

Whisk together cream, icing sugar, vanilla and cornstarch mixture until smooth. Heat in the top of a double boiler over hot water, whisking constantly until mixture thickens. Remove from heat, cover with plastic wrap and chill. Yields 1 cup.

Crème Anglaise:

1 cup whole milk
2 egg yolks
4 tablespoons icing sugar

Heat milk in the top of a double boiler over hot water. Whisk together yolks and icing sugar. Stir a small amount of the hot mixture into the yolks. Return yolks to hot mixture and cook gently until mixture lightly coats the back of a spoon. Remove from heat, cover with plastic wrap and chill. Yields 1 cup.

Each serving (including Crème Anglaise) contains:

Calories	*296*	*Protein*	*3.0g*
Carbohydrates	*48.5g*	*Total fats*	*11.5g*
			(Saturated fat 6.2g)

BLUEBERRY CLAFOUTTI

HALLIBURTON HOUSE INN

We are offering directions for making this pastry with a food processor. If a processor is unavailable, simply combine the flour, sugar and salt in a large bowl and rub in the butter. Incorporate the egg and roll into a large ball, then follow the instructions below.

Pastry:

1 1/3 cups flour
1/4 cup sugar
pinch salt
1/2 cup butter, cut in cubes
1 egg, slightly beaten

In the bowl of a food processor combine flour, sugar, salt and butter. Switch on and mix the ingredients until they are evenly distributed. Add the egg and continue to process until dough binds and comes away from the sides of the bowl. Roll into a ball and cover with plastic wrap. Chill 1 hour.

Preheat oven to 375°F. Roll pastry on a lightly floured surface or between two pieces of plastic wrap. Fit into a deep 9-inch pie plate and flute edges. Weight pastry with dried beans or rice. Bake 15 minutes, then remove weights. Return to oven until light brown, approximately 3 to 4 minutes. Remove from oven and cool.

Filling:

2 cups fresh blueberries (or other fresh fruit)
3 large eggs
1/2 cup sugar
1/4 cup milk
1/2 cup sour cream
1/2 teaspoon vanilla

Sprinkle blueberries into shell. Whisk eggs and sugar approximately 3 minutes, until pale yellow and thick. Gradually beat in milk, sour cream and vanilla. Carefully pour batter over berries and bake at 375°F for 30 to 35 minutes, until filling is set. Cover pastry edges with foil if necessary, to avoid overbrowning. Let stand 20 to 30 minutes before serving warm. Serves 6 to 8.

Each serving contains:

Calories	315	Protein	6.2g
Carbohydrates	40.7g	Total fats	14.7g
		(Saturated fat 8.0g)	

Blueberry Clafoutti ▶

BLOMIDON INN LEMON MOUSSE

BLOMIDON INN

*Innkeeper Donna Laceby tells us that they serve this delectable dessert a number of ways,
depending upon which fruits are in season. We offer the recipe with
fresh Maritime strawberries.*

4 eggs
2/3 cup sugar
1/3 cup butter
1/3 cup lemon juice
zest, finely grated, of 1 large lemon
1/4 cup lemon juice (second amount)
5 teaspoons unflavoured gelatin
1 1/4 cups plain, low-fat yoghurt
1 cup heavy cream (32% m.f.), whipped
1 quart fresh strawberries, rinsed, hulled and
    thinly sliced
sugar, to taste

In a large double boiler over hot water, stir together eggs, sugar, butter, lemon juice and zest. Cook, stirring constantly, until mixture thickens.

Place second amount of lemon juice in a small saucepan and sprinkle with gelatin. Place over medium heat and stir until gelatin dissolves. Stir into lemon mixture. Set aside to cool for approximately 30 minutes.

Stir yoghurt into lemon, then fold in whipped cream. Lightly grease a 9-inch springform pan, then line with clear plastic wrap. Pour lemon into pan and refrigerate several hours or overnight. Rinse and hull berries. Slice into a bowl and sweeten with sugar, if desired. To serve, carefully remove sides of pan, peel away plastic wrap and slice in wedges. Top with fresh strawberries or seasonal fruit of choice. Serves 8 to 10.

Each serving contains:

Calories	*249*	*Protein*	*5.7g*
Carbohydrates	*21.4g*	*Total fats*	*15.7g*
		(Saturated fat 9.1g)	

LEMON ANGELS ON RASPBERRY COULIS

CHEZ FRANÇOISE

This is a beautiful dessert with a nice contrast of colour. Prepare your coulis in advance to allow time for it to chill. The lemon dessert can be served warm from the oven, but is equally delicious when prepared early in the day and served cold.

1/4 cup butter
2/3 cup sugar
4 eggs, separated
2 tablespoons lemon zest
1/3 cup all-purpose flour
1 cup milk
1/2 cup lemon juice
pinch of salt

Preheat oven to 350°F. Cream butter with all but 2 tablespoons of the sugar. Beat in egg yolks and lemon zest. Stir in flour, then add milk and lemon juice. Beat egg whites with salt until light, then gradually add remaining sugar and beat until firm. Gently fold egg whites into lemon base. Spoon batter into a buttered 8-inch round baking dish. Set dish in a larger pan of very hot water and bake for 40 to 45 minutes. To serve, drizzle dessert plates with Raspberry Coulis and top with a large spoonful of the lemon dessert. Serves 6 to 8.

Raspberry Coulis *(supplied by authors):*

2 cups fresh or frozen raspberries
1/2 cup sugar, or to taste
1/4 cup water
2 teaspoons cornstarch, dissolved in 1
    tablespoon cold water
2 teaspoons fresh lemon juice

In a heavy saucepan over medium-high heat, bring raspberries, sugar and water to a boil, stirring occasionally, for 5 minutes. Prepare cornstarch mixture and stir into pan. Add lemon juice and simmer, 2 minutes, stirring constantly. Strain sauce, then chill until cold. Yields 1 cup.

Each serving contains:

Calories	*253*	*Protein*	*5.1g*
Carbohydrates	*40.1g*	*Total fats*	*9.0g*
		(Saturated fat 4.7g)	

EGG NOG ICE-CREAM IN CARAMEL CAGES

SEASONS IN THYME

Chef Stefan Czapalay of Seasons in Thyme Restaurant serves this wonderful homemade ice-cream in decorative "caramel cages." We are providing directions for you to prepare the ice cream in an electric ice cream maker. Since homemade ice-cream is very dense, you might want to soften it slightly by placing the container in the refrigerator 20 to 30 minutes before serving.

1 whole vanilla pod (1 teaspoon vanilla extract)
2 1/3 cups milk
1 1/2 cups heavy cream (32% m.f.)
12 egg yolks
1 2/3 cups water
1 1/2 cups sugar

Split vanilla pod and scrape out the seeds; add to the milk and cream and place in a large saucepan. Bring milk mixture to a boil over medium-high heat.

While milk is coming to a boil, place egg yolks in a blender and process. Gradually stir about 1 cup of the hot mixture into the beaten eggs and mix. Pour egg mixture into the hot milk, stirring constantly, and cook 1 minute. Remove from heat and set aside to cool. Remove vanilla pod and seeds. In the meantime, in a separate saucepan bring water and sugar to a full rolling boil. Reduce heat slightly and continue to boil until mixture thickens, approximately 30 minutes. Set aside to cool.

Combine sugar syrup with milk mixture and chill. Put mixture into an electric ice-cream machine, and follow manufacturer's instructions to process until fairly firm. For this process you will need a large bag of ice cubes and about 1 1/2 cups coarse salt. When machine stops running, transfer ice-cream to an 8-cup freezer container, allowing at least an inch of space at the top for expansion. Freeze 4 hours or overnight before serving. Yields 6 to 8 cups ice-cream.

Caramel Cages *(optional):*

2 tablespoons water
1 cup granulated sugar

Place water in a medium-sized saucepan and add sugar. Stir to combine and bring to a boil over medium-high heat, stirring occasionally. Using a candy thermometer, heat sugar to 305°F and immediately remove from burner.

In the meantime, spray the top of a round ladle with Pam and drizzle caramel into the ladle. As the syrup cools, slide the "cage" off the ladle and set aside. Repeat this procedure until you have 4 to 6 cages. Yields 4 to 6 cages.

Each 1/2 cup serving of ice cream contains:

Calories	*253*	*Protein*	*3.8g*
Carbohydrates	*33.8g*	*Total fats*	*12.0g*
			(Saturated fat 6.3g)

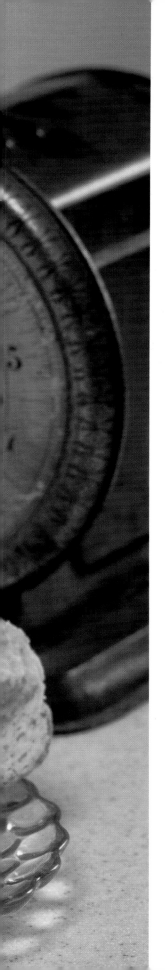

CONDIMENTS

The practice of preserving and pickling fruits and vegetables arose when our ancestors found that sweet, acidic or salty foods did not easily spoil. Today, our food supply is waiting at the supermarket where we can find even the most exotic produce in the depths of winter. Yet the colours, flavours and aromas of traditional preserving and pickling continue to live on, in what may be called "a labour of love."

Our chefs would like to offer you a variety of innovative jams, jellies, chutneys and pickles. Some recipes, like Rosehip Jam from Inn on the Lake, are old. And some, like the Planters' (Barracks) Gooseberry Chutney and Paradise Jelly, are new. All are infused with an exceptional flavour that will add new dimension to your meals.

◄ *Paradise Jelly*

PARADISE JELLY

ACACIA CROFT TEA ROOM AT THE PLANTERS' (BARRACKS) COUNTRY INN

Jenny Sheito of the Planters' (Barracks) Country Inn loves to experiment with the fruits and berries grown in the gardens of her inn. She readily admits, however, that the quince has been a challenge to her ingenuity. Her perseverence has created a hit with Paradise Jelly, which is indeed like looking at the world through rose coloured glasses.

12-15 medium-sized cydonia quince (may use combination of 10 quince and 3-5 red apples)
12 ounces cranberries
water
sugar

Wash quince in warm water and rub with a cloth or brush to remove fuzz. Dry, cut in quarters and remove seeds and stems. If using combination of quince and apples, prepare apples by quartering, seeding and stemming.

Place quince and cranberries in a large stainless-steel pot and barely cover with water. Bring to a boil, reduce heat slightly and cook for 15 to 20 minutes. When fruit starts to soften, break it down with a potato masher to release juice and colour. Remove from heat and cool.

Pour pulp into a jelly bag and hang overnight to extract juice. Lightly squeeze to obtain maximum amount of juice. Measure juice and return to pot. For each cup of juice, add 1 cup sugar and stir to combine. Bring to a boil, stirring until sugar is dissolved. Boil for another 10 to 15 minutes, until jelly reaches jelling point. Skim, pour jelly into hot, sterilized jars and seal. Yields 5 to 6 8-ounce jars.

Each tablespoon contains:

Calories	*48*	*Protein*	*0.1g*
Carbohydrates	*12.6g*	*Total fats*	*0.0g*

ROSEHIP JAM

INN ON THE LAKE

It is easy to see why our ancestors gathered rosehips and transformed them into vitamin-giving jams and jellies for the long Canadian winters. With its warm red colour and delicious flavour, this citrus flavoured version from Inn on the Lake is a true comfort food.

approximately 2 cups rosehips (enough to make 5 cups when combined with lemon and oranges)
1 large lemon
5 oranges
7 cups sugar
1 package fruit pectin (Certo)

Thoroughly wash rosehips and hull them (remove tips and tails). Thinly grate the peel of the lemon and two of the oranges, and reserve. Peel, seed, and chop the lemon and oranges. Combine chopped fruit and add enough rosehips to equal 5 cups. Process fruit in a food processor until liquid. (The seeds are very hard and will not break down.)

In a large heavy-bottomed pot, combine pureed fruit and sugar. Bring to a boil over medium heat, stirring constantly. Allow to cook at a full rolling boil for 1 minute. Remove from heat and stir in fruit pectin. Return to high heat and allow to boil for 3 minutes. Remove from heat, and press through a fine meshed sieve to remove seeds. Stir reserved zest into the jam, then immediately pour into hot sterilized jars and seal. Yields 5 to 6 8-ounce jars.

Each tablespoon contains:

Calories	*59*	*Protein*	*0.1g*
Carbohydrates	*15.8g*	*Total fats*	*0.0g*

GINGER PEAR HONEY

THE WHITMAN INN

Nancy Gurnham tells us this is a multi-purpose sauce. She serves it at breakfast with her French toast or waffles and as a dessert spooned over vanilla ice-cream.

6 pounds very ripe, good-quality pears,
    peeled, cored and sliced
1 tablespoon ground ginger
2 1/2 to 3 pounds sugar
3 lemons, zest and juice reserved

Purée pears in a food processor, then transfer to a large heavy-bottomed saucepan. Stir in ginger and sugar, cover, and let stand 24 hours at room temperature.

Stir in lemon juice and zest, bring to a boil, then reduce heat and simmer. Cook, stirring often until thickened, approximately 1 1/2 hours. Pour into sterilized jars and seal. Yields 5 to 6 8-ounce jars.

Each tablespoon contains:

Calories	63	*Protein*	*0.2g*
Carbohydrates	*16.5g*	*Total fats*	*0.1g*

SPICY TOMATO & APPLE CHUTNEY

BRAESIDE INN

This chutney has a marvellous flavour. You will want to make several batches when tomatoes are ripe and plentiful.

6 large vine-ripened tomatoes, peeled and
    chopped
6 medium apples, peeled, cored and chopped
4 onions, diced
4 cloves garlic, crushed
1 red or green pepper, diced
1 cup seedless raisins
1 lemon, zest and juice reserved
1 lime, zest and juice reserved
3 cups brown sugar
4 cups vinegar
2 tablespoons curry powder
1 teaspoon ground cardamon
2 teaspoons salt
1/4 teaspoon black pepper
1/4 teaspoon cloves
1/4 teaspoon nutmeg
1/4 teaspoon cinnamon

Remove skins from tomatoes. Place chopped tomatoes, apples, onions, garlic, pepper and raisins in a large kettle. Finely grate the rind from the lemon and lime and add to the pot. Squeeze the juice from the lemon and lime and add to all the remaining ingredients. Bring to a boil and simmer approximately 2 hours until mixture is dark brown in colour. Pour into sterilized jars, seal and store in a cool cupboard. Yields 7 to 8 8-ounce jars.

Each tablespoon contains:

Calories	23	*Protein*	*0.2g*
Carbohydrates	*6.3g*	*Total fats*	*0.1g*

GOOSEBERRY CHUTNEY

ACACIA CROFT TEA ROOM AT THE PLANTERS' (BARRACKS) COUNTRY INN

Jennie Sheito, innkeeper at the Planters' (Barracks) Country Inn, is well-known for her personally made condiments. A touch of cayenne pepper gives this gooseberry chutney a special hot flavour that is superb with meats.

2 pounds ripe gooseberries, topped and tailed
3 medium onions, chopped
2 apples, peeled, cored and chopped
2 cups raisins
2 cups brown sugar
4 cups white or cider vinegar
1 teaspoon mustard seed
2 tablespoons ground ginger
1/4 teaspoon tumeric
1 teaspoon salt
1/2 teaspoon cayenne pepper

Place all ingredients in a large heavy-bottomed pot and bring to a boil, stirring constantly. Reduce heat and simmer, stirring frequently until chutney is thick and smooth, approximately 1 to 1 1/2 hours. Pour into hot sterilized preserving jars and seal. Yields 5 to 6 8-ounce jars.

Each tablespoon contains:

Calories	29	*Protein*	*0.3g*
Carbohydrates	7.6g	*Total fats*	*0.1g*

FRESH FRUIT CHUTNEY

SUNSHINE CAFÉ

This chutney has a marvellous blend of spices and fruit. You might want to double or triple the recipe as it goes beautifully with a variety of dishes.

1/2 teaspoon whole allspice
1/2 teaspoon cloves
1/2 cinnamon stick
1/2 cup peaches, apples or pears, peeled, cored and diced
1/2 cup canned apricots, drained and diced
1 cup Mandarin orange segments, drained
1 cup cantaloupe or honeydew melon, peeled and diced
1 cup + 2 tablespoons sugar
3/4 cup cider vinegar
zest and juice of 1 orange
1/2 cup currants

Tie allspice, cloves and cinnamon stick in a cheesecloth bag. Combine all ingredients in a heavy-bottomed saucepan, bring to a boil and stir occasionally. Reduce heat and simmer for approximately 1 to1 1/2 hours, until thickened and dark in colour. Remove from heat and cool 10 minutes. Remove spice bag and puree chutney in a food processor. Pour into hot sterilized jars and store in refrigerator. Yields 1 1/2 to 2 cups.

Each tablespoon contains:

Calories	39	*Protein*	*0.5g*
Carbohydrates	10.3g	*Total fats*	*0.9g*

Gooseberry Chutney ▶

RED PEPPER & CORN RELISH

THE MARSHLANDS INN

For the faint of heart, we suggest using the lesser amount of hot pepper sauce. However, be advised that we tested the recipe using the full amount, and it was delightful!

1/3 large red bell pepper
1 tablespoon cider vinegar
1 tablespoon pure maple syrup
1/2 to 3/4 teaspoon hot pepper sauce
1/2 teaspoon ground tumeric
1/4 teaspoon salt
1 1/2 teaspoons vegetable oil
1 10-ounce package frozen corn, thawed and
   drained
2 tablespoons finely sliced green onions

Roast pepper under a broiler until blackened on skin side. Seal in a paper bag and let stand 10 minutes. Peel to discard blackened skin, then finely chop pepper.

Combine vinegar, maple syrup, hot pepper sauce, tumeric and salt in a bowl. Gradually whisk in oil. Stir in corn, red pepper and green onion; toss to coat. Cover and refrigerate several hours to blend flavours. Allow to stand at room temperature 30 minutes before serving. Serves 6.

Each serving contains:

Calories	*141*	*Protein*	*2.7g*
Carbohydrates	*23.3g*	*Total fats*	*4.7g*
		(Saturated fat 0.6g)	

FRESH INDIAN RELISH

BRAESIDE INN

You will want to serve this when tomatoes are abundant. The use of East Indian spices produces an exotic dish that will complement poultry or lamb.

1/2 medium red onion, shredded or grated
2 ripe tomatoes, thinly sliced
1 tablespoon vegetable oil
1 tablespoon cider vinegar
1/2 teaspoon dry mustard
1 teaspoon curry powder
1/2 teaspoon sugar
1/4 teaspoon ground cardamon
1/4 teaspoon garlic powder
1/8 teaspoon ground fennel
salt and pepper, to taste

Place tomatoes in a shallow bowl and cover with onion. Whisk together oil, vinegar and spices. Pour dressing over tomatoes and allow to marinate 1 hour. Serves 4.

Each serving contains:

Calories	*53*	*Protein*	*0.8g*
Carbohydrates	*5.3g*	*Total fats*	*3.7g*
		(Saturated fat 0.4g)	

Red Pepper & Corn Relish ▶

INDEX